CW00919946

Rough Diamond

Notes from a Big Island

George East

A First Impressions book

Rough Diamond

Published by La Puce Publications
Website: www.george-east.net

© George East 2022

Typesetting and design by Francesca Brooks

paperback edition ISBN: 978-1-908747-77-8
e-Pub version ISBN: 978-1-908747-76-1
kindle version ISBN: 978-1-908747-78-5

Other books by George East

Home & Dry in France
René & Me
French Letters
French Flea Bites
French Cricket
French Kisses
French Lessons
French Impressions: Brittany
French Impressions: The Loire Valley
French Impressions: The Dordogne River
French Impressions: Lower Normandy
150 Fabulous French Recipes
The Brittany Blogs
Home & Dry in Normandy (compilation)
French Kisses (compilation)
Love Letters to France
France and the French
A Year Behind Bars
Just a Pompey Boy (memoir)
The Naked Truth series
How to write a Best-Seller
The Naked Truth about Women
The Naked Truth about Dieting
The First Impressions series
A Balkan Summer
The Jack Mowgley Mysteries
Death Duty
Deadly Tide
Dead Money
Death á la Carte
Dead & Buried

LA PUCE PUBLICATIONS
e-mail: lapucepublications@hotmail.co.uk.
website: www.george-east.net

Contents

It's a curious fact that the Isle of Wight is at the same time one of the most-visited but least-known places in the United Kingdom. Contrary to what a lot of people who live on the mainland seem to think, it's not really the Island That Time Forgot, but it is subject to some weird misconceptions. Like that it's a foreign country with its own currency and language, or even that the locals have more than the normal finger count.

In *Rough Diamond*, George East gives his unique take on a fascinating and truly unique island which for many centuries has attracted royalty, scientists, inventors, philosophers, painters, poets and writers, revolutionaries, genuine eccentrics and also serious nutcases.

A best-selling travel writer, novelist and now disgraced nascent actor (see later), George admits responsibility for at least thirty books. After writing, eating and drinking their way around Europe for many years, he and his wife bought a home on the Isle of Wight. This is an honest account of their first impressions of an enchanting, magical if sometimes maligned and often misunderstood diamond of an island.

Author's Note

When I Googled loads of info-sites about the Isle of Wight, a not uncommon question was whether visitors would need to take their passports. Another asked if the currency was Euros and whether the inhabitants spoke English. Believe it or not, they were serious enquiries (I checked). Other references placed the Island anywhere from one to twenty miles off the south coast, and one relocated it to the North Sea.

Apart from the publisher's advance, the miasma of misconception about the Isle of Wight was why I wrote this book. When and if you finish it, I hope you may have a better idea about what this rough diamond of an island is really like. Or at least what *I* think it's really like. For sure, anywhere that has been a favoured getaway or home for a handful of kings and queens and a legion of poets, artists, scientists and great thinkers must have something going for it…

Fact and Fiction

I don't know why, but mocking or misrepresenting the Isle of Wight seems a favoured pastime across all sectors of society. The 'Queen of Mean' Ann Robinson casually averred recently that Henry VIII's favourite flagship *Mary Rose* didn't sink by accident off Portsmouth in 1545. The ship was actually scuttled by the crew, she claimed, just to avoid them having to visit the Isle of Wight.

Actress Emma Thompson even accused the Isle of Wight of birching wrongdoers. She got it wrong, and later apologised (she had meant the Isle of Man, she said), but her comments resulted in an avalanche of letters and calls to the Island's media outlets. Some really switched-on and tech-savvy Islanders even sent e-mails. Tellingly, most of the communications were not to complain about Ms Thompson's error, but to say what a splendid idea it would be to give the Island's young vandals and other miscreants a damn good thrashing.

Apart from being perceived as being stuck irretrievably in the past, the Isle of Wight is also a magnet for other inaccuracies, allegations and downright slanders. All the locals I have encountered have only one head and (mostly) ten fingers. Then there's the scurrilous assertion that when a caulkhead (someone born on the Island) introduces you to his wife and sister he may well be accompanied by only one person.

Whatever it was like in the past, the Island nowadays is anything but a closed community and immigration from the mainland has grown apace in recent times.

To dispose of another common calumny, the Isle of Wight is not God's waiting room. The average age of residents is 44 years, while in the rest of the UK it's 40. It's just that most of the incomers are of an age when they like to live at least partly in the past, and start checking out the best funeral plan packages.

Thinking about it, it seems to me that the main reason the Isle of Wight is subject to so many misconceptions and calumnies is simply because it's set apart from the rest of the Kingdom by a fairly wide stretch of water.

Up until the end of the last Ice Age (around 9000 years ago) it was just another bit of the mainland. In truth, the Solent channel is no more than a river that got bigger.

Evidence of human occupation predates the separation, and so rich is the Island in fossils and dinosaur remains that Stephen Spielberg considered setting the film Jurassic Park here.

Long before it became a popular bucket-and-spade holiday and retirement destination, early visitors and settlers included Celts, Romans and French raiding parties. The buying of a holiday home on the Island by Queen Victoria set a trend that continues to this day. The Empress and her consort's frequent and lengthy stays at Osborne House attracted a host of famous names and celebrity hangers-on who mostly loved what they saw.

It is also wrong to say the Island lives in the past. Lots of people who live here know that Harold

Wilson is no longer prime minister, and as recently as 1970 the Isle of Wight was the setting for the then largest rock festival ever held. Jimi Hendrix headlined and other performers included The Doors, Emerson Lake and Palmer and Joni Mitchell. Whatever your age or tastes, how's that for cool?

Perhaps another contributor to the feeling of apartness from the rest of the country is that, not so very long ago, the Isle of Wight was a kingdom in its own right.

In more recent times it was adjudged part of Hampshire until a 'home rule' campaign resulted in the Island becoming a ceremonial non-metropolitan county in 1974.

Another distinctive distinction is that the Isle of Wight is one of the biggest islands in the United Kingdom. At high tide it's also the smallest county in Britain. Roughly diamond-shaped, the Island covers around 147 square miles, with a population of 137,000, not counting pigs, sheep, cows, holidaymakers and sometimes notorious prisoners. This means only around 370 people share each square kilometre, while just across the Solent in Portsmouth the same area is crammed with more than 5000 bodies fighting for elbow-room, parking spaces and even air. The comparison becomes even more dramatic when you factor in that more than half the Island's population live in the seven main towns.

Things can get busy on the Island, though, and the population swells quite dramatically as more than two million visitors arrive each year, mainly during the summer season. As a recent study revealed, more than half of all domestic holidaymakers in

Great Britain have visited the Isle of Wight. The study did not reveal how many came back for a second visit.

Visitors who spend a lot of money and bugger off after a week or so are generally welcome. One of the more polite terms for any visitor or settler is 'overner', while only those born on the Island may be called 'caulkheads'. It's said the nickname comes from the ancient trade of caulking, or stuffing hemp into the seams of ships to make them watertight. It was an early but common slight in naval circles that any ship which took on water and foundered must have been caulked on the Island, and by someone with too many fingers to do the job properly.

Nowadays, caulkheads are an endangered species, though just a century or so ago were in the majority, it was said by locals then that the best way to test a resident's provenance was to tie him or her up in a sack and drop them in the Solent. If the sack floated, the person inside was a true caulkhead. If not, he or she was a foreigner and so no great loss.

∞∞∞∞

Disclaimer

To avoid upset, expensive legal action or physical confrontation, I would point out that all my opinions of the places and people encountered during my first year on the Isle of Wight are just that: Opinions. Some names have been changed where I did not want to cause offence or unpleasantness, especially in the form of a punch on the nose.

1

"This Island is a little Paradise"

Communist proponent, keen amateur hair and
beard grower and unashamed IOW fan, Karl Marx

We are on the move, and for once I don't want to go.

Since I caught and kept her, my wife and I have lived in several countries and under more than sixty roofs. This tally does not include short stay or holiday homes, squats or foreign prisons (a case of mistaken identity).

The rented premises have included the usual houses and apartments, but also more interesting and even exotic places such as former ice cream vans, drug dens, canal boats and, once, a former pig sty still partly occupied by the original tenants. By that I mean we shared a roof with four Basque sows and a thankfully not-too-wild boar called Descartes. My wife said it was the first time she had lived with a proper boar as well as an old ham.

Across the years we've also owned and lived in more than a score of homes in three countries, though not all at the same time. It's not that we like the process of buying and selling property, just to occasionally change what we see out of the window when we wake up each morning…and to know we own a little bit of what we see.

Or at least I do.

My ancestors were seafarers, Scottish Reivers and Irish travellers, which may help explain what my wife calls my itchy feet. It is true that after a while and wherever I find myself and how attractive is the environment, I fancy a move. Michael Palin once told me (and a couple of million other tv viewers) that he always wanted to be where he was not, and I know exactly what he meant. Luckily, my wife shares - or pretends to share - my enthusiasm for seeing what lies around the next corner.

Mostly those corners have been situated in what we Brits like to call 'abroad', but the birth of what will be our last grandchild recently persuaded us (or rather my wife has persuaded me) that we should set up home closer to our family in Portsmouth and watch Little Jack grow up. When he has become a surly teenager, she will agree to us fleeing across the Channel again. If I am still alive, of course.

Looking at the options, we knew we could not bear a move back to our home city. We will always love and fiercely defend Pompey, but after living in splendid isolation under the big skies of rural France, Bulgaria, Spain, Scotland and Wales, the idea of sharing a tiny island with another 200,000-odd (and some very odd) people was not beguiling.

But, my wife reminded me, there was another island close-by, and one which was fifteen times as big as Portsea Island and with far fewer (if sometimes odder) residents. All that separated it from the mainland was five miles of water and, as some would say, about a century in the attitude of the inhabitants.

Ironically, as she also pointed out, that narrow sleeve of sea water is both the Island's strength and weakness. People love visiting the Isle of Wight, but not the prospect of living there. Some because they believe they would feel cut-off and trapped, others because commuting to work every day without a jet-pack or helicopter would be impracticable. It is certainly true that the price of a return trip across the five miles between the Island and mainland can be dearer than a flight for two to Southern Spain.

That's another reason there are so many elderly people living on the Isle of Wight. They don't have to get out of bed and go to work each morning. Another attraction is that property is markedly cheaper than across the water, and the setting and scenery are stunning. The shortage of trendy night clubs, tanning salons and McKentucky, Nandos and Starbucks outlets is not a problem for those of mature years. For us (or at least me) there would be the bonus that the Isle of Wight is as close as we can get to France without living there, and if what we hear is even vaguely true, the culture and attitude (if not the food and wine) are somewhat similar.

Although I hate the idea of leaving France, I have to admit there should be rich pickings for a book about the Island if a tenth of what I have heard is remotely true. As her closing argument, my wife points out that I am used to writing about unusual and sometimes bizarre foreign countries, so our time on this most unusual of islands should be a bit of a busman's holiday.

~

My wife thinks she may have found our next home, and I am running out of excuses for staying on in France.

We have been renting a caravan without wheels which is masquerading as a holiday cottage at the western end of the Isle of Wight while Donella has been organising the search for somewhere to live more permanently. I've not been invited to take part, which may be because when she has left property-hunting to me we have usually paid a high and bitter price. I admit that I tend to go by first impression and gut reaction, and that sometimes this can cause sizeable issues to surface like Moby Dick appearing unexpectedly alongside the Pequod.

A good example was when we (or actually I) planned to set up a snail-farming business and live off the land at our first home in France. Because of an impulse buy and lack of attention to the details (except the giveaway price) by me we ended up with a one-bedroom cottage with not even a garden. As is not uncommon in France, every inch of the acre or so outside belonged to someone else, which the estate agent had forgotten to mention. Also, as is also not uncommon in rural France, the owner would rather die than sell us a square inch of the land his ancestors had worked, lived and died on.

Our next move was to a farmhouse and mill cottage on ten acres of woods and waterways in Normandy. The Mill of the Flea was really cheap and in a wonderfully bucolic setting, but sat alongside a madly fast and noisy road. We knew it would be a problem but made the trade-off because it was such a wonderful place to live, and in those days replacing vehicle-damaged hedges, fences and walls was relatively cheap.

When my wanderlust kicked in and it was time to move on, I found us a bargain-buy manor house with two each of kitchens, bathrooms and sitting rooms and more bedrooms than we could count. The property was surrounded by thousands of acres of brooding marshlands, of which a handful would be ours. It wasn't until we were woken at dawn on our first day as owners that we found the barns over the fence were actually improvised kennels housing seventy very excitable and loud dogs. As my wife likes to remind me, if you buy cheap and without doing your homework, there is usually a further price to pay.

~

After a month of fruitless searching, I'd begun to hope that Donella would get fed up and let us stay in Brittany. Then one morning she arrived in the Go For It! bar at Funland Bay Holiday Home Park waving a piece of paper like a particularly smug Neville Chamberlain.

'I think I've found it' she said.

'What,' I replied wittily, 'The Lost Chord or my right sock?'

'Neither. It's our next home. Maybe.'

'Where and What?' I asked a trifle waspishly. 'A log cabin in the middle of a forest with bears and wolves and sprites? A former smugglers lair on a cliff, with a secret passage down to the cove?'

'Nope,' she said. It's a nice little bungalow. With only a couple of near-neighbours. And it's in a cul-de-sac.'

I looked for any signs she had been at her favourite Loire rosé, then said: 'I trust you are either drunk or joking?'

I went on to point out that at the very top of our list of no-nos had been a bungalow. Only people waiting to die or with a really serious fear of heights lived in bungalows, didn't they? And we had agreed we would rather live on a main road with a traffic separating us from neighbours than at the end of a dead-end with people washing their cars and looking at ours disapprovingly and hearing our rows or me swearing and farting in the garden.

'Whoa.' She re-waved the piece of paper and said: 'Hold your horses till you get the full picture, mister. I've been looking at this place on Google earth.'

'And?'

The neighbour on one side is a small forest.'

'Oh. And?'

'And the back gate opens on to a bridle path.'

'You mean we'd have endless hen and stag nights and women in white dresses running by and chucking bouquets over the fence?'

'As you know very well, I said 'bridle', not 'bridal'. It's horses not brides that would be going by. And think of all that free fertilizer for the rhubarb.'

'What rhubarb?'

She smiled like a poker player lying down a card to complete a winning hand. 'On the other side of the track are shedloads of allotments, and I reckon one could have our name on it.' She paused for effect, then said: 'And there's more.'

I stopped fiddling with my mouse and looked up. 'Go on, then.'

'The track outside our back gate leads up to a country park with an old fort and miles of walks and woodland trails. From the top of the hill it looks as if you'd be able to see clear across the Island to the sea and Portsmouth. And there's loads of wildlife and even a big badger sett not fifty yards from the back gate.'

'Okay,' I said putting my hands up. You win. It must be worth a look. I suppose.'

'I'll give the agents a call now' she said. 'By the way, there's another couple of clinchers.'

'Go on,' I said. 'It's free?'

'No, but it's well within our budget.'

'And secondly?'

'The name of the country park outside the back gate is Golden Hill.'

'And?'

'And On Golden Hill would make a great title for a book about our first year here, don't you think?'

'Okay,' I said. 'Tell the agent we'd like a look, but I bet it's not all it's cracked up to be'.

~

Last Christmas I gave my wife a brand-new cement mixer. This year it's to be a new home. Unfortunately for me and my hopes of staying in France, 'Greenbanks' (yes, I know, but it could have been worse, like Home Lea or DunRoaming) almost lives up to the estate agency's enthusiastic details.

It is very much not the sort of place we are used to, but as bungalows go it was, well, a nice little bungalow and probably similar to a thousand other such buildings on the Island. It's an irony that bungalows are in demand in places awash with old people and thus at a premium, but generally get a bad press. When I told a friend Donella had arranged a viewing, she warned us about getting 'bungalow legs'. When I asked what she meant, she said that not having stairs to climb atrophied your legs over time. I think she had confused the facts that old people generally buy and live in bungalows because their lower limbs are not as spry as they were. It's not their single-storey home that gives them dodgy legs, just their age.

Having said that, I am not at all keen on the idea of living in a bungalow. No matter how big it might be, to me it seems as if someone has stolen the first floor. But what there is of the Lilliputian property is okay.

Up several concrete steps from a pocket handkerchief front garden and through the plastic front door lie a reasonably-sized sitting room, a small kitchen, shower room and two bedrooms pretending to be three.

In place of our usual wood-burning stove and flagged floor, Greenbanks offers double-glazing, central heating, fitted carpets and - as the estate agent pointed out, a double and detached garage with electronically assisted up-and-over doors. Wow. I suppose it is something to do with living in such an overcrowded country, but it is true that a double garage carries immensely more status than a single, especially if it not connected to the house.

This brick box would fit comfortably into the smallest of the ancient barns on our home in France, but as my wife would say, that is not the point. Property prices on this side of the Channel are what they are.

As claimed, the bungalow sits on a fairly green and definitely grassy bank at the end of a cul-de sac on the outskirts of the village of Freshwater. As estate agents would say (and ours did), the elevated setting affords views from the back garden of the nearby cliffs and downs named for Queen Victoria's favourite Poet Laureate. This, our man literally pointed out, was where Alfred Lord Tennyson liked to stroll while composing catchy little odes like *The Lady of Shallot* and *The Charge of the Light Brigade.*

Selfishly, we could have done without any neighbours (as no doubt most of ours would have felt after we moved in next door), but a house in splendid isolation even on the Isle of Wight would have been way beyond our means. In rural Normandy, a much more capacious single-storey farmhouse in fair nick and sitting in a hectare of land would be valued at around a quarter of the asking price for Greenbanks.

The horrendous cost of property in most of the UK is of course a major factor in why so many Brits choose to buy homes in France and Spain. They can own a place they could only dream of in Britain, even though it means living in a country they don't like.

Although there are bright and shiny and obviously frequently cleaned cars on the driveways here, I note with relief that none of the surrounding properties overlooks our prospective new home, and there is only one immediate neighbour. I am told they are elderly, have no dog and keep themselves to themselves. Over the low fence on the other side is, as Donella points out, what makes Greenbanks a bit special. A line of lofty oaks overhanging the garden marks the start of many acres of woodland - and a country park. Even better, the gate in the back fence opens onto the promised bridle path and swathe of allotments on the other side of the track.

Standing and admiring the view across the downs and the merest glimpse of sea, I heard a noise from a mixture of youthful chat and laughter and a familiar clatter. As I looked disapprovingly at the agent and my wife, a line of riding helmets containing youthful heads appeared above the fence. Each of the owners turned our way, smiled and waved a cheery greeting as they passed. Looking as if he was trying to decide whether this was a selling or negative point, the agent explained that the heads belonged to customers of a local riding school. They went by only a couple of times a day, and we could always make the back fence a bit higher if we didn't want them to be able to look down on us. A bonus, he said brightly, was that their passing meant there was always a good supply of fertilizer for the garden. I huffily said that my wife had already made that point, and it sounded as if they had been in collusion.

They exchanged glances and I saw that they had.

After he had gone, I looked around for any reasons for not being in favour of considering the place as a new home. Unfortunately, I couldn't think of one except, that Greenbanks is on the wrong side of the Channel for me. Unless I can come up with a persuasive argument for not moving to the Isle of Wight, it could be adieu France and hello Golden Hill.

~

Dusk falls swiftly as a wintry sun heads for the horizon and the waves making way for our ferry glister like quicksilver. Behind us is the tree-lined and mist-shrouded coastline of the Isle of Wight. Before us, a firmament of twinkling lights signals the loom of our home city of Portsmouth.

Whenever we have found a serious contender for a new place to live, the tradition is to go to the local pub or bar and discuss the pros and cons. When it has been my find, I try to avoid too many objections by getting my wife to look at the details through rosé-coloured glasses. In foreign climes, these meetings usually take place in an interesting bar in France, Spain, Portugal or Eastern Europe. On this occasion it's at the bar of the Wightlink ferry.

We have been this way many times, and the routine is invariable. If I am keen on the place, I will brush away the negatives and smooth over any objections, trying to paint a glowing picture of how our new home could be a paradise with a little money and work. If my wife is not in favour, I will be wasting my breath, but she knows I enjoy the exercise. If, on the other hand, she is keen on a property, she will simply list all the merits while disposing crisply of any negatives.

This time I find it hard to come up with any objections when she asked what I thought of Greenbanks.

'It was…okay,' I granted her.

'Glad it bowled you over,' she said dryly. 'So, what exactly wasn't to your liking?'

'You mean apart from it being a titchy bungalow in a cul-de-sac surrounded by the sort of people who clean their cars more often than I have a bath?'

'Most people clean their cars more often than you have a bath. In England we can't afford anywhere with no neighbours, and what's wrong with a bungalow?

'They're for old people'.

She looked at me with an odd expression. 'Well, in years you technically are old.'

'Bloody cheek,' I said. 'But what if we get bungalow legs?'

'What do you mean?'

'It's a well-known fact that people with bungalows lose the use of their legs by not having to go up and down stairs.'

'Rubbish. Anyway, there's a hundred acres of country park outside the back gate and the track goes uphill. And with no stairs you won't have to worry about falling down them while you're sleepwalking after too much Merlot and toasted Camembert.'

'That's another thing', I said, clutching at straws,' how will I live without my daily supply of Camembert?'

She smiled. 'I checked it out on-line and Lidl at Newport stocks the proper Norman stuff - and cheaper than you could buy it where it's made.'

'Ah.' I said, looking round for other more significant objections. 'But what about the cost of the ferry? Pounds per mile it must be the dearest in the world.'

'Quite possibly. But it's way cheaper than a Channel crossing, and residents get a very good discount deal. Next?'

I lifted my empty glass. 'Another slug and I might be able to come up with something.'

'Too late, the bar's closing and we'll be docking in a bit.'

She opened her bag, pulled out her phone and handed it to me.

I looked at it and then her: 'What?'

She smiled her sweetest smile. 'Phone the agent and put in a really low offer.'

'Why me?'

'If they take it, you'll be so pleased with yourself you'll forget your objections to living there.'

'But what if they don't? Does that mean we can go back to France?'

'Nope. We'll just keep looking.'

Seeing my face fall, she reached out and patted my knee. 'Cheer up. Remember, it's you who always wants to see round the next corner.'

'But what if there's nothing much worth seeing round the next corner?'

She smiled and shook her head. 'Just give the Island a chance and I think you'll find there's a lot more to the place than you think. And registering your first impressions of anywhere is what you do. From what I've read, you'll have lots to write about.'

Her expression softened, and she patted my knee again. And if you really, really hate it here, you can always rent somewhere across the Channel.'

'What about you?'

'I want to see our last grandchild grow up. When he leaves school and becomes a teenager, he won't want his smelly old grandparents hanging around. Then we can go back to your beloved France.'

I did some quick mental arithmetic and frowned. 'But by the time he's a teenager, I'll be eighty-something. If I make it.'

She stood up and put her arm through mine as if to help me to my feet. 'Oh, you'll make it alright. And if not, I'll scatter your ashes from the ferry as we dock at Cherbourg.'

∞ₒₒₒ∞

"The Isle of Wight is not Paradise. It is a rough diamond."

Award-winning poet and travel writer, Paul Hyland

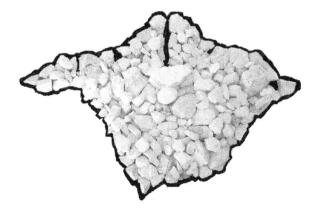

The 'Isle of White' map on the cover was designed and created by the very talented Islander Francesca Brooks. It was made with lumps of chalk garnered from across the Island, each piece cunningly positioned from whence it came. After the photographs the montage was disassembled and the components returned to where they had spent the previous few million years.

Lesmenez, Finistere, Brittany:

Dusk steals across the meadow and the creatures of the night begin to stir. I think I heard an owl hooting a moment ago, but it could be our nearest neighbour practicing his bird impressions. Old Alain only does owls, but is always a hit at the village senior citizens' monthly get-togethers.

Fairy lights twinkle on the lofty fir tree my wife planted as a tiny sapling to mark my 50th birthday. It spent its early years in Normandy and we brought it with us to our new home in Brittany. It is sadly too big now to take across the Channel when we leave, and like a lot of our fondest possessions will be staying in France. A good bit of my heart will stay with it.

It's Christmas Eve, and soon a party's-worth of friends and neighbours (not always the same thing) will be arriving for drinks and a buffet and, when enough apple brandy has been downed, a spot of Breton dancing. It's become a tradition of ours, but this year will also be a farewell party.

I'm sitting on a tree stump in a patch of woodland in the grounds of our home in Brittany, thinking about what we are leaving behind at what may be our last home in France. Our original plan was to live here for a year while I wrote a book about the region, but this place of magic and myth cast its spell on us and we stayed for three. Had it not been for the arrival of little Jack, I could have stayed here forever. Or at least that's what I tell myself now I know we are moving.

Brittany is officially part of France, but not

according to the majority of Bretons. The region is very Celtic, and has its own tonsil-twisting language. Most Bretons speak their language on a daily basis and French is very much a second language. My wife has Breton ancestors and I feel at home here for many reasons. As well as the space, freedom and easy-going culture, it is almost a criminal offence to cook a dish without butter or cream. Another reason is that Bretons brew good cider and beer and take their drinking seriously. Elsewhere in France, bars may have hooks on the front of the counters for ladies to hang their handbags on. In our quayside local they are for customers who fall under the spell of the ferocious apple brandy and need a little help to remain upright

Unless something dramatic ensues, the removal van will arrive in less than a week. Donella is in the final stages of packing and re-packing, and I have been sent outside to tidy up the acre or so of woodland and garden. Beyond that is the lake which, to be truthful is more of a big pond.

My chainsaw lies contentedly puttering alongside my tree-stump seat, and the corpse of a fifty-foot pine is alongside. When I have finished my coffee, the trunk will be sliced into rings and then split into logs. They are to be a present from me to the new occupants of our home, and the activity, as my wife said, keeps me from under her feet. The logs are not much of a present as pine burns in a flash, but the tree needed to come down and using it as firewood is the best and most respectful way of getting rid of it.

Sadly, my chainsaw will not be coming with us, nor the cement mixer, log splitter or twelve-bore shotgun.

They would not be much use where we are going, but our parting will hopefully not be permanent. Along with some of the more massive furniture, six hens, two goats and an ill-tempered rabbit, the majority of our goods and chattels will be spread around the barns and spare rooms of friends in Brittany and Normandy, waiting our return. At least, that's the plan.

I take a swig of apple brandy-laced Breton coffee and look around me. Although I like to be on the move, I shall miss our home and the little hamlet and most of the people who live here. And few would argue that it is a place of rugged beauty that anyone with a soul for Nature in all her variety would find hard to leave. But to be fair, moving on is what I like to do and three years is a long time for us to stay in one place. But what a place it is.

Halfway up what they choose to call a mountain in Brittany and built at least two centuries before I was born, the rambling farmhouse sits at the bottom of a track leading up to thousands of acres of lofty moorland, pierced with giant shards of granite.

The main house is more than spacious, and the bungalow in the Isle of Wight would almost fit into the massive main room. The two-feet thick bare granite walls hold up the massive beams which support the ceiling, and the stone-slabbed floor shines with a patina resulting from the attention of a dozen generation of wooden clogs. One end of the room is taken up with a massive fireplace which is home to a Godot wood-burning stove and a family of mice. Beyond the main room, a vast kitchen looks out past the huddle of barns and towards the big, tree-lined pond.

A door from the kitchen leads down stone steps to a bathroom which has running water down the walls as well as from the taps. It is said to be so damp because a stream runs under it and in the old days it would have been a very convenient convenience. Upstairs are four bedrooms and a second bathroom. And there's quite a bit more. Next door is a very badly-done gite which even in France would fall foul of basic Health and Safety accommodation requirements.

It is a commentary on the relative values we and the French put on the places where we live that this rambling and enchanting property, its lake and woodlands and all the land surrounding it is valued at fifty thousand pounds less than we are paying for the modest bungalow on the Isle of Wight.

Unless, that is, I win a last-minute reprieve.

~

'So, I'm not the only one to miss a small problem with a property we intend buying, then? Like it's falling down?'

I'm trying not to look smug as we sit in our local bar, discussing a phone call that came while Donella was packing her waist-length waders. The fish pond in the back garden of the bungalow is only about a foot deep, but she says the waders are sure to come in handy.

The call had come from the surveyor we'd engaged to give the bungalow on the Isle of Wight a basic once-over. Ironically when considering the state and age of some of the properties we'd bought on either side of the Channel, this was the first surveyor we'd employed. In rural France, paying someone to look at a house and tell you what was wrong with it was generally considered a waste of money. After all, any fool could see when a roof was missing or a chimney pot or gable end wall about to topple. And the general if illogical feeling was that if a building had been standing for two centuries or more, it was not going to collapse in the new owner's lifetime.

As my wife reported, the surveyor had called to say he was in the garage at Greenbanks, and wondered if we wished to call the survey off. She had asked why and he had asked if we had not noticed the rather large fissure in the floor. She had responded that I had not bothered to inspect the inside of the garage, while she had noted the crack but didn't think it was that serious. That, she had pointed out pointedly, was why we were paying him to tell us of any serious problems. Obviously given to sarcasm, the surveyor had agreed that it was not big enough to lose a bicycle or even a small child down at the moment, but was certainly serious as far as the likely longevity of the garage was concerned.

'So did you tell him to call the survey off?' I asked, scenting a last-minute reprieve from the prospect of having to leave our lovely home here.

'No,' she said. 'I told him to go ahead and finish it.'

'Why?' I asked, which I thought was a reasonable question.

'Well,' she said, 'the place has everything we want in a lovely location, and we'll never find one like it. We're not going to be living in the garage, and we've lived in places with a lot more wrong with them than a crack in the garage floor. Anyway, it's a great bargaining point.'

'Bargaining point?'

She took a moment to signal to the barman for another glass of full-strength Breton cider for me, then said: 'All you have to do is show the surveyor's report to the owners and say we'll only go ahead if they knock the cost of replacing the garage off the agreed price.

'And how much is a new, double garage?'

'No idea, 'she said. 'But it will be a good bit I reckon. And we may not need to spend it on a new garage.'

'What, you mean you'll just let it fall down and leave the rubble there?'

'No of course not. But the surveyor didn't say it would fall down anytime soon. He said it could fall down. If that happens and they take our lower offer, we'll have the money to build a new garage.'

'And if it doesn't fall down in our lifetime?' I asked, seeing where she was coming from.

'We'll have bought a very cheap bungalow, even by Isle of Wight standards.'

'But you do realise that when we want to go back to France we'll have a bit of a job selling a place with a collapsing garage?'

'Ah', she said, reaching for her glass of pommeau, 'I hadn't thought of that.'

I looked thoughtfully at her and took another sip of cider. Unlike me, my wife is a bad liar, which I think is because she has had nowhere near as much practice as I.

∞∞∞∞

3

"...it was nine weeks of horrid interruption of all work."

Naturalist Charles Darwin's testy comment after an extended stay at Freshwater in 1868 when he was supposed to be getting on with *On the Origin of Species*.

Artists and smuggler's delight: Freshwater Bay

Despite my machinations, it looks as if it is going to be *au revoir* to France, and *Helletun* (Wightean for 'hello') Isle of Wight.

When I told a London-based friend where we were going, he looked askance and asked why on earth we would want to live in such a dump. When I asked if he'd been to the Island, he shrugged and said no, but he knew people who had and they called it the Isle of Shite. He actually shuddered as he added that he'd heard that the locals regarded white socks and even legwarmers to be the cutting edge of fashion.

Shite or Wight and for good or ill but for hopefully not too long, we are installed at Greenbanks. The metaphorical and actual dust is settling and the garage is still intact. After some brisk negotiations, the owners accepted our much-reduced offer, so you could say we got a bargain buy. Perhaps not if you are the type to worry about your posh double garage being likely to implode at any time, but it is a concern my wife is happy to live with. So am I - if I can persuade her to let me use the money we saved to buy a wreck in France.

After the journey of several hundred miles and across two stretches of water, our goods and chattels are mostly unpacked. As usual, the house-moving sprite has been at work though this time we have only lost or mislaid a dozen items. They range in size and value from an oyster-opening kit to a non-working Breton short-case clock, and bizarrely, an antique Breton wardrobe that converts into a place in which to sleep.

A potential drawback with living at the end of cul-de-sacs is that while eliminating the disturbance of passing traffic, full-frontal positioning and proximity mean thoughtful neighbours are a must. It is said that good fences make good neighbours, but that was before televisions, sound systems and even grass strimmers could reach the approximate decibel level of a Saturn V rocket lifting off from the Kennedy Space Centre. We did a surreptitious check on who lived in the houses closest to our new home before putting in the offer, but you can't tell much by walking past with an imaginary dog or ringing bells and pretending you have called at the wrong address. Estate agents are unlikely to spill the beans if there's a homicidal maniac living nearby, and we know from experience there's always a risk of inheriting Freddy Krueger as a neighbour.

So far, though, all seems okay or at least acceptable. Directly over the fence is an identical bungalow to ours, where live an elderly couple. They have no dogs or cats, noisy children, motorbikes or any apparent penchant for staging raves or wife-swapping orgies. Jack and Mary are from London, seeing out their years in this quietest of corners of the Island. We were invited into their home on moving day, and first impressions were good.

I think we have struck lucky, and if we have to have neighbours, I don't think we could have done much better. Jack has a quick, dry wit and is obviously fond of banter and verbal sparring. Mary is a pleasant soul and makes onion chutney to die for. We have already adopted our relative positions and roles, and I will play my larger-than-life part, while Jack will treat me as if I am a likeable but regrettable relative. He is naturally a small, slight man, but looks painfully thin and that a strong wind from the nearby Needles would bowl him over.

We will try to be good neighbours, which to our minds is pretending not to be here but being ready to help if the need arises.

~

Golden Hill Country Park sits above the village and stretches across thirty acres of woodland and walks with glorious views to the Solent and beyond. It was a training ground for the military from the 19th century and the fort is one of Lord Palmerston's string of defences against Napoleonic invasion. Similarly rotund and unappetising concrete structures lie along the north-western coast of the Island and in the Solent waters. None fired a shot in anger, and were consequently dubbed as Palmerston's Follies.

Ironically, the land-based forts where soldiers once lived in dank and grim conditions are now expensive designer-style apartments and maisonettes, and some of those in the Solent are advertised as 'boutique' hotels. That anyone should want to pay to stay in them would surely raise a ghostly wail of disbelief from the shades of Victorian squaddies once billeted there.

Though we have heard distant shotguns, the country park is a haven for wildlife, many of whom have begun to visit us. Since setting up the bird feeders, we've become a popular diner for robins and blackbirds, magpies, fearless flights of sparrows, pigeons, tits and buntings, crows and seagulls, normally reclusive jays and occasionally a glittering appearance from an almost iridescent green woodpecker. From the woods comes the hoarse screech of pheasants, and we are regularly treated to a fly-past of formations of swans, geese and ducks and the solitary heron heading for the nearby river.

Remarkably and unlike human tribes, they all seem to rub along regardless of size and species and a confrontation is rare.

At night the silence is regularly broken with the bark and squeal of foxes and the irritable snuffling and grunting of badgers. They are of course the arch beasts of the woods, immensely strong for their size and totally fearless. We have yet to meet the extended family which lives a short distance along the track from our back gate, but I am sure my wife will find a way to entice them into the garden. Hopefully she will also seduce the red squirrels which are another mark of distinction for the Island.

Because of the Solent, the Island is deer-less since the last pair were hunted to death. Another anomaly is the colour of the squirrels here. For ten thousand years, all squirrels in Britain were red. Then the Victorians introduced the larger and more assertive grey variety from North America. I don't know who or how they did the counting, but there are said to be 2.5 million greys compared with only140,000 reds. They are to be found in some numbers in Scotland and Wales, and a smattering in England. Population will depend on the size of available woodland, and the coverage on the Island means around 3,500 reds can call the Isle of Wight home. Red squirrels build their nests or dreys of leaves and moss and twigs high in suitable trees. They usually build more than one home so they can move about, and survive the winter by burying caches of nuts. They need to bury more than they will need, as they are absent-minded and often forget where they have left them. They swim well and, like us, are either right or left-handed. They can live up to six years. The bad news for our chance of making our garden a regular haunt is that squirrels cannot absorb tannin, so the tens of thousands of acorns the woodland next door are off the menu.

~

There's a network of foot and bridle paths linking the village to outlying hamlets, and horses, dogs and their riders and walkers pass our gate from dawn to dusk. I suppose the odd drug or drink-fuelled rave or dogging session may take place in the woods during the warmer months, but the age demographics suggest they will not be big or noisy events, and any dogging activity will more likely be of the walkies variety. Overall and from what I have seen so far, I have to admit that this could be a pleasant place to eke out one's remaining years. France still sends siren calls across the Channel, but it looks as if there may be a threat to unrestricted travel to our second favourite country. Or anywhere else in the world.

According to the doom-laden reports, we are threatened with what some over-excitable media outlets are already calling a Doomsday Plague. The latest pandemic scare to add to Avian Flu and Mad Cow Disease is thought to originate in China, who of course brought the world SARS or Severe Acute Respiratory Syndrome. The latest pandemic panic will hopefully turn out to be a false alarm, though will inevitably cause a dramatic over-reaction. In France when Avian Flu arrived, some of our neighbours took to hiding their chickens in the house in case a helicopter flew overhead in search of those who were flouting the quarantine rules. During the Mad Cow madness, British visitors to France were banned from bringing in cheese sandwiches and even tins of corned beef.

Reports on the new virus says that the best defence is keeping a safe distance from others. Given how it's almost compulsory to shake hands and kiss even strangers in France, I can see social distancing being a big problem there. If there is to be a new plague, I suppose a small island with natural social distancing of acres rather than metres will not be a bad place to live.

∞∞∞∞

I'm guessing, but I reckon at least half of all picture postcards of the Isle of Wight will feature some part of the Island where we live. There might not be much going on in West Wight, but in parts it is almost lip-smackingly photogenic.

Bucket, sand and spade holiday diversions like amusement arcades and piers are to be found to the north and east, and that's where the great majority of the population gather. The major towns of Newport and Ryde and resorts like Shanklin and Sandown account for three-quarters of the Island's residents and attract many of the millions of visitors a year.

At this end of the Island, it's another story and almost another world. Home to long-held family farms, fiefdoms, ancient castles and ancient burial mounds, West Wight is a place of soaring white cliffs and emerald green, rolling downs dotted with villages awash with thatched cottages.

Once upon a time this part of the coastline was a regular haunt of smugglers; according to some, it still is. But nowadays it's outdoor types who are drawn to the combination of forest and coastal walks and undulating cycling challenges. The shallow waters, long tides and prevailing south-westerly winds are a magnet for those who like surfing and kite-boarding, while the heady heights of chalk cliffs are a perfect launch pad for hang gliders and, sadly, the rare individual who chooses to take a leap into oblivion.

Freshwater Bay is actually a modestly-sized, sheltered cove with a short stretch of pebbly beach overseen by the high downland named for Victoria's favourite Poet Laureate. Around the corner, out of sight from the land and cut off at high tide are a series of caves once favoured by smugglers with tobacco, brandy and other desirable contraband from France.

~

Compared to the wild and empty beauty of the coastal area, I suspect the fondest of residents would not claim Freshwater village to be a pretty place. In fact and if there were such a contest, I reckon it would be in line for the ugliest village on the Island.

This is due to a combination of factors. One is the slow death of individual, small businesses which inevitably followed changing times, increased mobility and the arrival of the cheaper, all-under-one-roof supermarkets. Consequently, the main street is home to at least a dozen drab, sad and eyeless shop fronts, occupied briefly by people who think they have a good idea for a new business and are soon proved wrong.

But some outlets do prosper, and most of them are aimed at those losing their mobility, eyesight, hearing and teeth along with their short-term memories. There's an impossibly long waiting list to become patients of the two dentists (who tellingly specialise in denture making and fitting) and both opticians are busy when their customers can find their way to them. Within hobbling distance of the car park are a foot care clinic and a mobility shop, its window filled with walking sticks and Zimmer frames, scooters, incontinence aids and sinister-looking appliances with lengths of rubber tubes and squeeze bulbs.

They say the number of charity shops in any high street are an inverse measure of prosperity and there are four in the high street. What they offer is also a good indicator of the average age and inclinations of their customers. Tennis racquets and track suits and mini-gyms are rare, while cotton trousers with elasticised waistbands and tea sets featuring kittens abound.

On the plus side, there's an excellent local bakery,

butcher's shop and that rarest of local enterprises, a wet fish shop. There's also an excellent library with obliging staff a zig-zagging ramp for mobility scooters, a surfeit of large-print and audio books and lively competition for a free read of the national newspapers.

Further evidence of popularity with retirees of this part of the Island is that the windows of the four estate agencies make a feature of bungalows and ground floor apartments.

Like other coastal areas with much natural beauty and little industry apart from tourism, this part of the Island also seems to appeal to creatively-inclined types. This inclination may be expressed by the pursuit of painting, writing books and poems, or making music, uncomfortable furniture from driftwood and jewellery from seashells. Others prefer to work creatively on themselves, with eccentric hairstyles, facial hair and clothing that the most easy-going charity shop would refuse as a donation. As my wife says, this lack of sartorial concern and convention means I will feel as at home here as in France most *profonde*.

A depressing commentary on modern times is the number of people who drive through the village on their way to somewhere else. This is because Freshwater is a funnel for virtually every vehicle heading eastwards. This means a constant, fast-flowing and noisy river of cars, motor cycles, vans and lorries making crossing the road a risk for all but the most nimble and erasing any sense of villageness. It's hard to stand and pass the time of day when you can't hear yourself speak.

In spite of this, Freshwater is a pleasant enough

place, and, unlike some of the more upmarket coastal villages on the Island, nearly all the people with homes here live in them full time.

~

A grey, clammy day, with a mantle of mist laying insouciantly over Tennyson Down. This means visibility will be poor on the coastal waters, confirmed by the disappointingly high-pitched squeak of the Needles foghorn. It sounds every fifteen seconds when conditions are bad, which in winter is often. I'm told by a local music teacher that, since the lighthouse became automated, the pitch of the horn has risen from a manly middle to a shrill top 'C'. As he observed, from a musicological and practical perspective, foghorns should sound as deep and mournful as the fate that awaits any ships that come too close. Perhaps, he added, it was part of the cuts that they could no longer afford a proper, grown-up foghorn.

~

Our back garden is a pot-holed morass, proof that the Badger Concordat is not working.

In France, badgers are not protected and in some parts *Blaireau au Sang* is still seen as a culinary delicacy. That means, as with any remotely edible animal, they tend to be rare on the ground. When Donella learned of the sprawling colony which has made its home up the track from our back gate she was enchanted. I was not so sure.

The line of what looks like sand dunes in which children have been digging tunnels stretches along one side of the track and comes to within fifty yards of our back gate.

This might sound a treat to naïve wildlife lovers, but there are drawbacks.

Generally speaking, badgers like to stay where they have set up home, but if they find somewhere more interesting, they may decide to move. If they decide your garden is nicer than where they are, you may find yourself with squatters. This is not good as their setts are protected by law, and I have read horror stories about electrical circuits being eaten, sewage pipes blocked and broken, and even houses collapsing. I heard yesterday that some bodies have been dug up and moved to another part the churchyard which sits beside the Yar river because a badger family decided it would be a nice place to live.

Technically, badgers are short-legged omnivores and part of the same family as polecats, weasels and ferrets. The European badger is the largest of the species and can grow to the size of a small pig. They have strong, sharp teeth and powerful claws for digging, and have no natural predator except Man. Nocturnal, they can run at 20 mph, and are omnivorous, accounting for the lack of hedgehogs and rabbits in the vicinity of our sett. Their main diet is earthworms, which accounts for our back garden looking like a miniaturised version of a WWI battlefield model.

When we moved in, I listened to the advice of the Badger Fanatic Society, who said that their nocturnal visits were inevitable so we should enjoy them. If we filled in the holes in the fence which were their shortcut they would just make new ones.

They were literally unstoppable, so the best approach was to embrace them. Not literally but spiritually, and if we fed them well with peanuts - which they preferred even to earthworms - they would not need to excavate our garden.

Basically, the BFS were wrong. Or they lied. The more we fed the nocturnal visitors, the more they dug for worms. A hungry badger can get through seven hundred earthworms a night, and it seems as if our offerings have been seen as no more than an appetiser.

As there seemed no way of stopping them arriving each night, I tried offering a delivery service. As I explained by speaking loudly down the bigger burrows, I would arrive with their supper every evening after dark as long as they kept out of our garden. They should feel free to explore other people's gardens, and if it helped I would paint a cross on our back door to show it should be passed by.

Now that they have broken the terms of my proposal, I have to come up with a new plan. If I simply stop putting food out at night in the woods, the foxes will suffer. If I invite the foxes into our garden, the badgers will be sure to beat them to it.

Last week I phoned a Cornish farmer friend and he said the best way was to gas the burrows or poison the food I was so inexplicably giving them. When I said that sounded a bit drastic and was anyway against the law of the land, he shrugged verbally then said there was another possible solution. He had not tried it himself as he had a big dog and a shotgun, but he had heard that badgers had a strong and even sensitive sense of smell. There was an old country belief that they did not like and could be repelled by the odour of male urine. It had to be stale, he added, and the staler the better.

I waited for a moment for the punchline, then realised he was serious.

'Are you telling me I've got to mark my boundaries like some sort of demented tom cat?'

Another verbal shrug over the line, then: 'Well you can try. Most animals can be frightened off by the scent of a superior enemy. I have heard that lion's poo is best of all, but I think your pee will be easier and a lot cheaper.'

~

Don't tell my wife, but Freshwater is beginning to grow on me.

One of the reasons I like living in foreign parts is that they do things differently. Though we are technically still on British soil, some things here are done very differently, and, like rural France, unusual people are thick on the ground. It's not just that the Island can seem to be backward rather than forward looking; it's more than that, and perhaps something to do with being surrounded by water. All islands seem to attract people who are a little different from the norm, and some a great deal different. We have not moved to The Island of Doctor Moreau, but there are some similarities.

~

The next phase of my wife's plan to put down roots here is a visit to the parish council offices to go on the waiting list for one of the allotment plots across the track outside our back gate. We're told by insiders that there's a long wait and some people are said to have grown too old to lift a spade by the time their names have come up. There's also the problem that, though demand increases as growing-your-own has become trendy, the allotment is now half the size it was. Abandoned huts and overgrown plots sit morosely behind a fence because some distant authority, probably under the advisement of the Badger Fanatic Society, decided the occupants of the sett might be put out by people digging up their earthworms.

Next-door neighbours: The giant badger sett on Golden Hill

The local primary school sits alongside the track down to the village from our back gate, and passing by is like a distant memory made real.

All Saints is a truly old-fashioned primary school, housed in a group of sturdy Victorian flint buildings with church-type arched windows. Nods to the current century take the form of satellite dishes, basketball hoops and parking spaces, but this is still essentially a place of the past. Memories flood back each time I hear the timeless playground chatter and gleeful whoops before the vigorous ringing of a hand bell summons the infants back to the real world. Last time I went by there was not a mobile phone in sight, and I swear a group of children were playing at Cowboys and Indians, or as we must say nowadays, Cowboys and Native Americans.

~

I can't find any historical references, but it's a fair bet that Freshwater is named for the ditch posing as a stream which runs alongside the road through the village. The western river Yar (there is another one to the east of the Island) surfaces near the beach in the bay and joins the estuary at the end of which sits the very posh yachtie and well-heeled second-home owners haven of Yarmouth. Along with what must be the most decrepit public toilets in the area and a cheering lack of graffiti, the village offers a genuine gem of a lurking place for people like me.

In the way that some people can't pass a cake shop or pub, I have bookshop constipation. The more unusual and obviously unprofitable the business, the better, and the one in our village is a classic which could surely only survive elsewhere in a twee area of North London or Ross-on-Wye.

In a blessed antidote to a world of big-name chain stores which have adapted to appeal to modern tastes for bland uniformity, Mrs Middleton's bookshop and café is a pure, perfect one-off. The windows and shelves are stacked with books by a dazzling range of proper and popular writers, with Voltaire and Balzac co-existing Jilly Cooper, Lee Childs, Madhur Jaffrey and Jeffrey Archer. Inside, you can get a cup of tea or coffee while sampling a book and buy or leave it when you go. Most importantly, the tea comes in proper teapots with proper thin-walled and heavily-patterned porcelain teacups. Although the eponymous middle-aged owner is usually to hand, she employs a delightful lady of advanced years who is an upmarket version of Julie Walter's ancient waitress who spills the soup before making it to the customers' table.

~

While not exactly in the Vicar of Dibley class for characters, the parish council members and headquarters seem pleasingly parochial and in some cases eccentric.

The offices lie on the upper floor at the back of the village hall, and an interesting provision is made for visitors unable to make it up the stairs. It is an open lift which looks like an indoor version of one of those hydraulic platforms used by people who mend telephone lines or pick fruit from tall trees. I couldn't resist it, and my wife watched in resignation as I climbed over the safety railing, repeatedly pressed the button and so caused it to grind to a halt between floors.

After taking pot luck on the doors and gate-crashing rehearsals of the Freshwater Amdram society and a lady adjusting her dress in a toilet, we found the comfortably dishevelled office and were made welcome.

The nice lady in charge of allotments said there are thirty people on the waiting list, but some of them may have moved, got fed up with waiting or died.

I tried not to look hopeful that the hand of the Grim Reaper could push us up the waiting list, and said there seemed to be a number of neglected or even abandoned plots apart from the badger territory. She explained that she had only just taken over the job and was going to check that all the plots were being worked. As with the waiting list, it could be that plot-holders may have lost interest, got too old to manage them, or passed on. I said we had noticed some suspicious-looking mounds on some plots which could indicate a cheap burial alternative, but I don't think she got my weak joke.

~

We are in shock, or as close to shock as we get after half a lifetime of receiving the occasional googly from the spin bowler of Fate.

On the way back from our meeting with the allotment lady, we noticed a shop which seemed to be suffering from an identity crisis. The main window was crammed with hundreds of Lego and superhero figures under the supervision of a full-size Spiderman hanging upside-down from the ceiling. Legions of model soldiers and space explorers jostled for room, while the other window featured a cute doll's house and a selection of embroidered cushions and clearly home-made knitwear. A notice on the door explained that it was a cash-only business, and inside, we could see shelves supporting jars of old-fashioned sweet jars, souvenirs, haberdashery items and mounds of knitting wool. Elsewhere were art materials and racks of clothing and, high on a wall, a display of ice hockey boots, sticks, masks, padded guards and what looked like a protective box. As with me and bookshops, my wife has a problem passing anywhere that sells wool, so we entered.

The late middle-aged lady owner made us coffee and explained that the ice hockey equipment had belonged to her husband, a leading player. He had been considerably older than her and had died some years ago. She kept the urn containing his ashes close to her, and had taken him on holiday on a number of occasions.

When she asked if we were visitors, my wife said we had just moved in to a house at the top of the village. When she heard which road, the lady's face clouded over and she asked if we knew about the new housing development on our doorstep. When I spluttered coffee down my shirt front, she said that two hundred homes were to be built in the fields alongside the allotments. The old school was also going to be closed and probably sold off for additional new housing.

As we got up to leave, she almost casually mentioned that, from what she had heard, the access route to and from the new estate would be running through our cul-de-sac.

Bite-size Island

History: Owned by a Norman family until 1293 and once a kingdom in its own right

Status today: A county since 1890

Distance from mainland: 4 miles

Total population: 139,000

Population density: 3.6 persons per hectare

Total land area: 147 square miles/380 km2

Ethnicity: 97.3 percent White, 1.1 Asian, 0.2 black, 0.1 other.

Age: 26 percent of the population are over 65, 15 percent 14 or under. The IOW has (but only just) a higher proportion of older people and a lower proportion of young people than the average in England and Wales

Households: 65,000

Household occupation: 2.3 persons per household. One in six households is occupied by a lone person of 65 plus.

One in ten houses on the Island stands empty.

4000 households are occupied by a lone parent with dependent children.

The Island has the sixth worse divorce rate in country

Towns
and (approximate) populations

Ryde	26,000
Newport	25,000
Cowes	10,000
Shanklin	8,000
Ventnor	7.000
East Cowes	6,000
Sandown	5,000
Brading	2,000
Yarmouth	1,000

4

Sign of the Times: Going Upmarket

"Hpǽr íu til stéorset?"

This invaluable phrase for any traveller caught short in foreign parts is Wightean for 'Where is the toilet?' Wightean is a satisfyingly eccentric tongue, composed in the mid-1970s by a resident who thought the Island should have its own language. In fact, it does in dialect terms, but more of that later. I'm told Wightean is a mixture of Anglo-Saxon, Maltese and Old Swedish with the word order in the Dutch form. I'm also told that up to five people are believed to speak or understand it.

It's strange for us to live in a place of such contrasts, where urbanity does not so much meet as collide head-on with countryside. We've always lived either in a built-up area or in splendid isolation, but this time we have almost literally a foot in both camps.

Beyond the front windows and through the Regency-style, plastic front door complete with spy-hole there sit rows of almost identical, neat and somehow smug-looking bungalows, outside of which lie shiny cars and manicured pavements. At our backs and, Narnia-like accessed through a single door, miles of mostly untrammelled rurality offer their delightful embrace.

It's barely dawn on a cold and clammy morning, and the mist hangs low in the tunnel of overhanging branches leading the way up to Golden Hill. A busy byway for horse riders and dog owners as well as badgers has made the track a muddy walk, but all around are signs that a new season is on its way.

A finalist in the Tourist Board's 'Welcome to the Isle of Wight' poster competition.

Variously known as lords and ladies, devils and angels, Adam and Eve or even snake's head, cuckoo pint is a plant which thrives in the damp shady environment. Delicate snowdrops, weedy daffodils, Siberian squill, crocuses and creeping myrtle also make a living here. There's always lots of horse shit, which is welcome, and dog shit, which is not.

It would be fine by me if owners just kicked their pets' 'love nuggets' (I actually saw their turds called that on a dog fanciers' website) to the side of the track, but why do they bag them up and then hang them like Christmas presents from tree and bush branches? Can you imagine what it would be like if horse riders did that?

Just before the start of the badger sett, I catch the signature aroma of a high-end French restaurant and spot a promising patch of bear garlic. We like the flavour it gives to salads and stews, and some claim it can, like dandelions, also lower cholesterol and hypertension levels. As an infusion it's said to repel cats, and I make a mental note to knock up a super-strong solution and try it as a supplementary badger repellent.

Through the mist I see movement near one of the holes and think at first it is a resident who has stayed out too late and is scurrying to the dark comfort of its burrow. Like Count Dracula, badgers don't like daylight.

Then I see the creature is a shaggy, cross-breed dog, sniffing at the entrance to one of the larger tunnels. I hope for its sake it does not investigate further. Badgers have very sharp and strong claws and don't take kindly to being disturbed.

As I warn the dog, off, its owner appears from a winding path through the woodland. She is wearing a mask and gives me a fearful look and overtly wide berth as she scurries past. Although I think she is over-reacting, it's a reminder that I and probably half the world took the threat of the pandemic too lightly.

Despite my and their early scepticism, the pandemic is emerging as a real threat, and experts are calling for a range of measures from shutting shops and pubs down to abandoning sporting events and even curfews or lockdowns. If it does prove as serious as some pundits are forecasting, I think this sparsely populated corner of an island off the mainland coast will not be such a bad place to hunker down.

~

I'm in a proper caff (as against something called a café bar or coffee house) with a mug of tea and Full English breakfast to work on while catching up on the week's news from around the Island. After decades of writing for them and sometimes appearing in them, I know that local papers are the same, with the same different stories. The events they report on may not be of much interest to the greater world, but they are a joy and it will be a tragedy to lose them. The Isle of Wight does well for coverage of local events, scandals and dramas, and there are several on-line as well as proper paper titles. There's always something happening on the Island, and this week the editor of the leading local paper has found enough worthwhile stories to fill nearly a hundred pages.

Two of them list recent planning applications, and I'm relieved to see that none seek permission to stick a couple of hundred houses in the field near our new home.

The more newsworthy stories include an 87-year-old lady who is touching her toes a hundred times for charity, and a musician who has released three new albums in a month despite the total failure of his previous offerings.

'I love every single one,' he says, 'they are fantastic and should all be massive hits, but unfortunately I'm the only one who thinks so.'

I admire his tenacity. As I have found in life, we can't all be good at what we would like to be good at, but it's the trying that counts.

Passing Traffic: Riders on Golden Hill

If challenged, I couldn't choose between the delights of dawn and dusk walks on Golden Hill. They are the times when the fewest people and the most members of the wildlife community are out and about, and I feel measurably closest to nature. I'm fine with people in their natural habitat of towns and villages, but when in the countryside I selfishly want it all to myself.

This morning I saw that the harbingers of spring have come to our garden as well as beyond it. There is a certain symmetry as well as contrast between the formal and natural and I delight in both. Before reaching the back gate I was assailed by the colours and fragrances of a dozen bushes and plants waking from their winter rest. There was a bewitching combination of clematis, Japanese honeysuckle, winter jasmine, mimosa two varieties of camelia, sloe, hydrangea, bay and variegated oregano, blackthorn, slender deutzia and common comfrey.

Altogether it makes for a cacophony of aroma and colour, and there will be much more to come as the year gets into full swing.

I wish it were otherwise but we can take no credit for this display of creative understanding. The previous owner of Greenbanks is no longer of this earth, but her hard work and care has left a delightful legacy and we are truly grateful. As Tennyson's successor Alfred Austin said, to nurture a garden is to feed not only the body but the soul. As Kipling said, Gardens are not made by singing 'Oh how beautiful' while sitting in the shade.

~

The structural surveyor's report on the garage has arrived, and tells us what was pretty obvious even to the untrained eye.

Basically, the report reports that the fissures across the floor are there because the garage has moved, and may or may not be still moving. The cause could be damage from the roots of the nearest trees or a problem of general subsidence.

The garage, like the house, was built on a slope, and over some war-time concrete buildings. The earth is also an unusual mix of clay and sand and chalk.

The report concludes with an informal assessment that the outbuilding could fall down tomorrow, next year, or given our age, not within our lifetime

~

Arriving on the track this afternoon I thought it was snowing. Then I realised that it was in a storm of dandelion seeds, using the breeze to spread their progeny far and wide.

Unless you are someone who wants their lawn to look like the baize on a freshly brushed snooker table and sees them as a curse, dandelions are one of nature's great gifts to humanity. The name comes from the French for 'lion's tooth', but they are commonly known there as *pis-en-lit*, or 'piss-the-bed.' This is because of the diuretic effect of the leaves, but according to countryside lore the plant has many more uses. They were and are believed to benefit digestion and help treat acne, liver disease and even cancer. They are of course, also much admired by rabbits. Dandelions are also a source of vitamins and the soluble fibre which helps maintain healthy bacteria in the gut. Some people dry the roots and make an infusion from them, but I have to say the drink is not my cup of tea.

The invasion does, however, suggest a possible business venture. Having seen how remorselessly they are taking over our back garden, and given the median age of Islanders, creating a diuretic drink called, say, Pee-Free could make another nice little supplement to the East family income.

~

I would not want to be thought of as some sort of ancient hippy tree-hugger, but I have struck up a friendship with a dead oak.

Just off the track leading to the old fort, it lies like a fallen warrior, and despite its prone position I feel it has an air of dignity. Were it badly damaged or rotting, I think I would react differently, but the body and branches are whole and the ivy makes it look still in leaf. In a way it appears to be just resting. The earth-covered roots reach towards the sky, and I could fancy that a giant hand could pick it up and replant and revive it. I know it's silly, but having talked myself into believing that it still lives, I feel neglectful if I do not greet it each day.

My new friend also lies at a convenient resting place and the bole is at a very comfortable height. I like to sit there, hidden from the track as I take a coffee while musing on life and death and pronouncing my views on matters of great or modest import. I have found that Ent is an attentive listener and never disagrees with my point of view, which makes a change from home.

I also like to see the reaction of some dog walkers when they feel my presence and turn to see a strange old man in a beret and sawn-off trousers sitting gnome-like on and talking to a dead tree.

Expensive holes in the water: Yarmouth mariner

While Freshwater is the biggest village on the Island, Yarmouth is the smallest town. At around a thousand residents it is, in fact, the smallest town in the United Kingdom.

Once upon a time, Yarmouth was a busy trading, fishing and smuggling centre. It's alleged that at one time every other resident was involved in the importing and selling of what they believed should be duty-free goods. Even in the ultra-respectable town as it is today, the old trade is whispered to be ongoing, but in different commodities. Not long ago, a local fisherman had an unusual catch when he hauled up one of his lobster pots and found a hold-all bag attached to it. Inside and neatly bagged up were several kilograms of cocaine.

Obviously aware of its status and desirability, Yarmouth sits smugly on the coast just a mile or so as the river flows from Freshwater. In other respects, the two are light years apart. A key indicator is the eye-watering cost of even a modest home in sniffing distance of the shore at Yarmouth. If you can actually see the sea and the property is old, quirkily built and sits in a cobbled street with a satisfactorily salty name, it will have a value and price seemingly beyond its weight in rubies.

Apart from when the hordes of summer visitors or unashamed rubberneckers descend, the narrow streets and characterful cottages lining them are often almost eerily quiet. This may be because so many are owned by people who don't live in them or need to let them out to others. A recent report revealed that one in ten domestic properties on the Island are second or holiday homes. I wouldn't mind betting that the ratio is a good bit higher in Yarmouth.

~

Another indicator of the up-markedness of Yarmouth lies in the sort and size of boats rubbing shoulders in the marina. Some of the gin palaces and yachts are bigger and better-appointed than our bungalow.

Unsurprisingly the pubs are very much gastro, and a lobster dinner for four could set you back the average Wightean's weekly wage. That there is not a single kebab, Chinese or Indian curry house is another indicator as to where Yarmouth is coming from. There is a high-church bakery, deli and provisions store for discerning customers, but all Yarmouthians have to travel to Freshwater for more common-or-garden supermarket items or Biryani or Peking Duck dinner for two.

Further evidence of how the place and people see themselves is the profusion of galleries where even a print by a local artist can cost more than many people in Freshwater pay for their cars. Then there's the ultimate symbol of sophisticated trendiness which is the antiquarian bookshop. It offers a re-binding and repair service, but I bet they don't get many punters calling in to get their copy of Fifty Shades of Grey spruced up.

A reminder that Yarmouth is more than a village comes with the pocket-sized but impressive 18th - century town hall. Our village hall has a weekly indoor market which is mostly old ladies selling old books and unwanted gee-gaws; Yarmouth town hall holds regular expositions showing off the talents of members of the local painting club.

Though now sensibly named for where it sits, Yarmouth has got through eleven identities since the first settlement appeared. At the time of Ethelred the Unready's 10th-century tax records it was known as Eremue, or The Place of the Muddy Estuary. The Normans laid out the grid system of thoroughfares, and the castle was built in the last year of the reign of Henry VIII.

Unkind critics have said that Yarmouth is like an oversized model village or a town which has been shrunk to fit the available space. This may be so, but the compressed jumble of grand and humble Georgian and Victorian styles is undeniably pleasing to the eye. It is more so because, unlike Old Portsmouth, Yarmouth was never bombed and thus did not have to suffer the indignity of implants of post-war cubist dwellings in the gaps.

The walk from the square along the waterside abounds with names like Pinings Corner and Loveshore Lane, and the mix and even muddle of types of architecture are extreme. Lofty Regency piles look down on once-humble fishermen's cottages, and my favourite looks like it was the inspiration for a setting in the Harry Potter films. The studded gate opens to a walkway with an arched verdigris-green copper cover. A flat-fronted and otherwise pristine building is fitted with apparently original early nineteenth-century windows. Attached to one side is what looks like a concrete castle folly devised by a Victorian moneyed madman. The castle bit has crenellations and there are oversized and delightful sugar-twist Tudor-style chimneys. Overall, it's the sort of home I fear I would quickly abandon my principles to make my own.

Although I claim to abhor tweeness, privilege and the air of superiority that comes with the smell and showing-off of serious wealth, the truth is that I am just plain jealous. I find Yarmouth and its location and mantle of wealth irresistibly appealing and would love to live or have a home here if I could learn the trick of making much more money than we spend.

~

There is an estimable coffee and cake venue at the start of the old pier, but we enjoy the coffee, conversation and home-made bread pudding at the takeaway close to where the ferry from Lymington arrives.

It is called Nammet and when we first visited and found the owner was from Portsmouth, I asked if she was married to a Turk. When she asked why I said there were lots of Turkish-run cafes in Portsmouth with the owner having married a local girl. She looked at me for a moment, then said she was single and although it might sound Turkish, 'Nammet' was actually Wightean for a light meal or snack.

~

Leaving Nammet, we turn away from the sea, go off-piste and find ourselves in a narrow thoroughfare rejoicing in the name of Seapie Terrace. Outside the tiny, terraced cottages are the usual suspects of old chimney pots, wagon wheels, black-painted ploughs and even a horse trough aglow with a dazzling winter floral display. Against it lies a period delivery bicycle with a huge wicker basket at the front. As we muse on how rich people like to own the places and display the things that poor people used to live in and use, one of the doors opens.

I brace myself for an unwelcoming scowl, but the elderly man smiles and asks how we are doing. We get to talking and he tells us we have met one of the few caulkheads remaining on the Island and probably the only one still living in Yarmouth. Like his father, he was born in Christmas Cottage and will die there.

His wife summons him to Sunday lunch, and before obeying he waves an encompassing arm at the terrace and says that when he was a boy every house was lived in by someone local. Now and including Christmas Cottage, there are only four properties not owned by overners and used only as holiday homes. It's funny, he says as we leave, how some people can't afford one roof over their heads while some can afford to have several.

~

Another day, another funeral company touting through the letterbox to be the ones to handle our passing.

I don't know if it's the Covid Crisis or the advanced age of most people who live in bungalows, but we are continually receiving special offers of anything from a cheap and cheerful cremation or the full monty of a 'natural' woodland burial in a beautifully landscaped area (drinks buffet and entertainment quotes on request). Then there's the bonus of a free gift of a pen or carriage clock.

The daily blandishments would be dryly amusing had we not just heard that our next-door neighbour is facing the end of his journey through life.

Jack's wife told Donella yesterday that he is not well, and would not be getting better. He is so thin his skin appears transparent, and something is clearly eating away at him.

Mary said that her husband had been having treatment for bowel cancer for a year or more, and the malignancy had moved into his liver. The specialists had given no forecasts, but said she must prepare herself for what was to come.

The news came as a grim reminder that, in the midst of the Covid crisis, life - and death - goes on.

~

Dusk falls and I am in search of a singing partner.

This is the time of year when the south of England is visited by a most unusual bird. Nightingales like to keep to themselves, so thick woodland makes for perfect nesting territory for nightingales. They also like to sing with vigour and would be classed as noisy neighbours under European Union specifications. Nightingales have been recorded singing at up to 95 decibels, and 87 is the limit of what the EU considers an acceptable noise level.

The name goes back a thousand years and means 'night songstress' in Old English.

Most importantly, nightingales are, as they say in bird-spotting circles, 'collaborative'. This means they will actually sing along with humans or even a musical instrument if it takes their fancy. This evening I shall settle down with my fallen tree friend and a flask of tomato soup and hope to tempt any nearby nightingale into forming a duet.

Unfortunately, as my wife says, I am tone deaf and cannot carry the simplest melody. I am barred from joining in at any carol service or even funeral where audience participation is encouraged, so it would be especially nice to find a partner who isn't put off by my abuse of the tonic sol-fa scale.

~

'Good morning,' said the lady.

'Oh, er, um, hello,' I replied, as naturally as one can when peeing on a hole in a fence.

'Cold enough for you?' she queried.

'Erm, yes.' (sound of a zip being hastily pulled up, followed by a squeal of pain as it catches on something small and soft on route).

The above is a roughly accurate transcript of my passing conversation with a middle-aged lady sitting on a horse of at least seventeen hands. I know this as, unless she was over six feet tall, she had to be astride a hunter-sized horse to be able to see over our back fence and down to where she had caught me in the act.

The lady's cheeks were glowing red, but more I fancy from exposure to the weather than embarrassment at finding me peeing on the badgers' favourite entry port. Being a horsey type, she will have seen much more than I have on show, and it is me who is feeling small and embarrassed.

The hole in the fence between back garden and woodland is almost exactly symmetrical, tunnel-shaped and just the right size for a burly badger. I have tried nailing boards across the hole, but as well as torn away they were broken into pieces as if the invaders were expressing their contempt for my feeble efforts.

Next, I placed a heavy garden slab over the hole and wedged in place with a large stone from the rock garden. I came out the next morning to find the slab broken and the rock at the bottom of the slope as if our visitors had been enjoying a bit of impromptu bowling practice. It was obvious that, short of installing a miniature Berlin Wall or prison-style electric fence barriers, normal preventative measures would not keep them out.

It was, I figured, time to follow one of my farmer friend's recommendations. For legal and humane reasons, gassing, shooting or poisoning are not an option. A small box of Lion Roar manure repellent came in at a pricey £14, but I did have an infinite supply of urine. Easy to produce and best of all, completely free.

That's how I came to be spraying the badger entry point as the head of the ruddy-faced lady appeared above the back fence as she clomped by on the bridal path. Given how cold it is and however good her eyesight is, I doubt she would have seen much from her vantage point, but perhaps I will in future use a plastic spray gun rather than the direct method.

~

More news about developments in and around the village, and, like the curate's egg it is only good in parts.

Spoiled for choice in a charity shop looking for suitable pairs of thin cotton trousers of the sort favoured by colour-blind elderly ladies, I recognised the woman serving behind the counter as a parish councillor.

When I explained that the trousers were not for personal use, she gave me an 'Oh Yeah?' sort of look and said what I got up to on a Saturday evening was my business. Then she asked how we were settling in and said she had heard that we were getting close to the top of the allotment list. If enough people surrendered their plots or died, we could be offered one very soon.

'That's if they haven't been built over,' I said gloomily.

She asked what I meant, and I said we had heard about the plans to build hundreds of executive homes in the fields beyond the allotments. Then there was the rumour that the primary school on our doorstep was to be closed and turned into another housing estate.

She smiled, and said that the thing about any village was that there were always rumours, and, by definition, rumours are usually very inaccurate. It might be allegations that a new resident was a former Nazi concentration camp Commandant, or that the local vicar was actually the Grand Ram of a Sex-and-Satan cabal. Sometimes the stories had an element of truth to them, though any former camp Commandant would obviously have to be ancient even by Freshwater standards. As to the Sex-and-Satan cabal, she couldn't possibly comment.

The proposal for hundreds of new houses beyond the allotments was a fact, she said, but the result of a governmental request for ideas and proposals to help the 'regeneration' of the Island. Unsurprisingly, the knee-jerk reaction by the main Island council invariably involved the idea of building lots more homes. The major mainland property developers were, also unsurprisingly, always keen to concrete the nicer parts of the Island over and throw up 'executive' homes that young couples would never be able to afford. But it was just a suggestion and not an application.

'So, it won't happen?' I asked

'Let's say it's unlikely,' she said, almost winking as she folded and slipped the polka- dotted trousers into a bag and handed it over like a barber passing over something for the weekend. 'The village,' she added, 'would be dead against it, and so would the parish council.'

'And the plans for the school?'

She looked thoughtful, then said: 'Ah, that's a bit more complicated.'

There was, she explained, a grant of several million pounds on offer for a new-build primary school which would accommodate pupils from the originally Catholic-run All Saints at Freshwater and the Church of England primary school at Yarmouth. By far the most primary-school age children lived in Freshwater, though some went to Yarmouth, which was smaller and had no playing fields.

'So, what's the problem?' I asked. 'If the majority of kids live in Freshwater and this site is bigger and better, why would the new place not be built here?'

She smiled again. 'You are a newcomer. Yarmouth parents would shudder at the thought of having to deliver their children to what they like to call the cultural desert of Freshwater.

'Even so…' I protested.

'Even so,' she echoed, 'there's a saying round here

that whatever Yarmouth wants, Yarmouth gets. And you know what they say about how money talks.'

'I've heard it,' I said. 'So what would happen to our school if Yarmouth gets what they want?'

She looked sympathetic. 'Well, in spite of the playing fields and surroundings it's not a greenfield site, so it could become yet another housing estate.'

I thanked her, paid for my trousers and asked her a final question:

'But the allotments are safe from being made into new homes?'

She smiled. 'Yep. The parish council owns them, and they won't be going. Unless the badger colony moves in of course.'

~

No duets with nightingales so far, but a bemusing only-on-the-Isle-of-Wight encounter after dark.

Walking up the track to serve the badgers and foxes a light supper, I saw a light moving around at just above ground level near my friend the fallen tree.

There, I found a small man on his knees and inspecting the trunk of the giant oak as he poked at it with a metal rod. Mutual introductions revealed that his name is Julian and he lives in the village.

As he went on to explain, he was looking for any species of myriapod. As I would know, myriapods are noted for having lots of legs, and there are more than 15,000 species. Millipedes and centipedes are obvious examples he said as he showed me a jar containing some wriggly examples.

'Like caterpillars, then?' I asked, just to show interest.

'No,' he said with a twitch of an eyebrow and a small sigh as if he had been asked the question too many times. 'Caterpillars are insects.'

'Ah,' I said, wondering how many people would be standing in a forest at the dead of night talking with a stranger about the differences between creatures with lots of legs. 'So what about woodlice? They've got a lot of legs.'

Again the twitch of the eyebrow and half-sigh. 'Woodlice are crustaceans.'

'You mean like crabs and lobsters?'

'Sort of,' he said, then went on to explain that there were more than three thousand species of woodlice in the world, thirty or more of them to be found in the United Kingdom. 'They like,' he concluded, 'damp, dark places and decaying wood.'

'Ah,' I said again, 'And your myriapod thingies only come out at night?'

'No,' he said rather pointedly, 'It's just that there are usually less people around at this time.'

I took the hint and wished him good hunting. As I turned to go, he nodded at the fallen warrior and said: 'It's funny how this tree has been down for a long time but shows no sign of decay. It's almost as if it were still alive.'

'Yes,' I replied, 'I often think that.'

∞∞∞∞

5

"She thinks of nothing but the Isle of Wight, and she calls it 'The Island' as if there were no other island in the world."

Maria and Julia mocking their cousin Fanny in Jane Austen's *Mansfield Park*

New life is everywhere as the good earth blooms. Except, that is, for the bare patch where the badgers have dug up the dozens of daffodil bulbs I planted outside the back gate.

As the scrape marks confirm, along with earthworms, cockchafers, leatherjackets and the odd hedgehog, badgers are very partial to bulbs. Having set up my pee-drenched boundaries, I don't begrudge them the bulbs as long as they refrain from turning our back garden into an ideal venue for mud-wrestling matches

~

We are asked to believe that a butterfly flexing its wings in New Mexico can cause a hurricane in China; but who would have guessed that someone eating a bat could put the world into stasis?

Although we have a better infection record than almost anywhere in the country, the Island is in partial lockdown, though it is hard to see the difference from the norm. The shops are mostly open, we don't go in for eating out at gastro-pub or even coffee shop prices, and would not want to be members of any social groups and clubs that would admit us.

In the village, the most noticeable effect has been to rewind time by several decades. The traffic has dropped to almost a trickle and most people are obviously, and as advised, staying safe indoors. All the older residents who venture out to the bakery, butcher's or supermarket wear masks, their eyes cautious and even fearful.

Most of the young people who live in the area don't seem too concerned with social distancing or mask-wearing. We are told that if they become infected it will just be like a dose of 'flu. We oldies and other vulnerable people could die, which understandably has an effect on our contrasting reactions.

Overall, there is an air of bemusement that this should happen and the classic sci-fi film and book scenario become real. Things have changed almost overnight, and I suspect some will stay changed.

One interesting aspect of the new norm is how individuals react to the situation, particularly in the type and of face mask they choose.

Designer jewel-encrusted or animal faced masks are understandably rare in our community. Curiously, so as are the full-face plastic shields as favoured by surgeons and welders. It is as if people prefer do not trust the transparency and feel safer not showing their faces. The situation has reminded me of how much we can tell about a person by their expressions. The eyes may be the window to the soul, but I have already found that ironic comments and throwaway lines can be seriously misinterpreted without a smile to go with them.

The standard issue masks are not cheap, and as ever inventive and cost-conscious, my one-time seamstress wife has been experimenting with a selection of face-coverings. An early design used the cups of her old brassieres, but when I modelled it on the Internet some wag said I looked like a right tit. Having turned down my suggestion of making use of my old underpants, Donella hit on what I think could be a winner if properly marketed. This was the reason for my scouring the local charity shops for old ladies' lightweight trousers.

Donella's designer masks are in effect tubes with elasticated tops made from the legs of the brightly-patterned cotton trews. They can be worn in the manner of a neckerchief, and pulled up to cover mouth and nose when necessary. Mine is red with white polka dots and wearing it, I fancy myself looking like John Wayne on a cattle drive across a dusty plain. My wife says I actually look like an old man wearing a mask made from a pair of elderly lady's trousers. Whatever the effect, my new mask is easy to wear and use, and I tried it out this morning to pick up a newspaper from a shop owned by Edward G Robinson.

That is of course not his name, but he is a dead ringer for the veteran Hollywood star in his final movie, Soylent Green.

The owner is a short, rotund gentleman of advanced years, and like Edward G in the film, he favours a neat white beard a close-fitting beret and an expression of resigned sagacity.

I don't know if the beret is a nod towards his artistic leanings, but more than half the premises is devoted to art supplies. A couple of steps away from the newspapers, greetings cards and sweets and shrimp nets is a world of charcoal pencils, sketch pads, brushes and oil and acrylic paints. The windows are also filled with paintings by local artists.

I have never seen anyone buy a picture, or anything in the arty half of the shop, and wonder if the owner stocks them for his own pleasure and simply because he can. I have also never seen him serve in the shop, but he likes to sit in a corner with his back to the front door, perhaps thinking of past days and paintings. Whatever his motives, he and his family and their shop add to and enhance the delightful differentness of this unusual village.

'I see no eagles': the hide at Newtown

As with English inns and bridges, any town with the prefix 'New' is usually very old. Don't ask me why, it's just an historical fact.

A few miles to the east of Yarmouth is a good example. Once the *de facto* capital of the Island, Newtown has, in a nice way, an almost post-apocalyptic air. It's obvious that there was a lot going on here once, but not now.

Standing alone near the shore like a sentry with nothing to do is a very fetching town hall which has no town to go with it. There is a rather pretty church and a gaggle of very desirable cottages up the road a bit, and looking at the narrow creek and glutinous stretches of mud they overlook, it's hard to believe that ships of up to five hundred tons once regularly docked here.

Nowadays a handful of yachts are the only craft to be seen, and they don't look as if they get out and about much. Not so long ago, the residents of this tucked-away little corner of the Island would be busy with fishing, managing their oyster beds and salt pans, and, of course, smuggling.

For some reason, Newtown seems more than quiet. It's less than a mile from what counts as a busy road on the Island, but the trickling creeks, endless expanses of glittering mud and thickly wooded coastline lend an air of utter tranquillity. Also, and of all hamlets I know here, Newtown seems to exist in a world of its own.

~

In medieval times the settlement was known as Francheville ('Freetown') and was probably founded well before the Norman Conquest. The old names of

Gold and Silver Streets show what rich expectations and values were attached to a place where honest trading and smuggling worked hand-in-hand. Some idea of the level of duty avoidance in the Island as a whole can be gathered from the fact that in 1840 alone it was reckoned that a hundred thousand casks of spirits passed through the central distribution centre of Rookley. And that was more than likely a serious underestimate.

The location of Newtown made it a perfect site for salt works and oyster beds as well as smuggling, and the townspeople gave thanks for their good fortune during a three-day festival dedicated to St Mary Magdalene.

Things changed when the Great Plague arrived, followed by a French raid in 1377 which mostly destroyed the town. A contemporary explanation of its demise is a localised version of The Pied Piper of Hamelin. The story goes that the townspeople paid a magical figure to lure the plague-carrying rats away and into the Solent. When they welched on the deal to pay his £50 fee, he picked up his pipe again and led all the children away.

Regardless of myth and legend, the long, often dramatic and bloody history of this little place has left its mark. For me, there's something special in the air and particularly in the woods bordering the mudflats. The silence is broken only by the wind soughing through the trees and the screams and caws of birds. Now and then as dusk falls, I am sure I have heard the creak of muffled rowlocks, a salty curse and the whiff of good French brandy. If it is true that moments of the past do echo across time, I think they can be heard in Newtown.

A carving on the church at Newtown

Coming out from the woods and on to the shoreline I stand and inhale the still beauty of it all. In the middle distance some rolling downland with stunted, wind-bent trees stretching along the ridge. Nearer to, the sun glints off the slow-moving waters and rich, dark mud, pierced by the skeletons of ancient landing stages, groynes and long-dead boats.

A wooden jetty stretches out from the shore to a wooden bird hide, silhouetted against the afternoon sun. I shift the stone holding the door shut, lift the viewing flaps and the framing of the panorama intensifies the monochromatic beauty. It lifts my cynical heart to see that there are two sets of binoculars on a shelf, and next to them an expensive-looking guide book to bird species. On the mainland and maybe even elsewhere on the Island they would be long gone.

I see that the book is open at the page featuring a rare and magnificent creature.

The white-tailed or sea eagle is the largest bird of prey to be found in Britain, and has a wingspan of up to 240cm (nearly eight feet). Their preferred diet is mostly fish, but they will go for lambs and (it was claimed) small children, which helps explain why they were shot to near-extinction at the beginning of the 20th century.

The breed was re-introduced to Scotland in 1975, and last year and despite the protests of sheep farmers, four were released at a secret location in the Isle of Wight. They promptly flew across the Solent to the mainland but are said to have returned and set up home in Newtown. If they do choose to stay here, you can see why. Not many sheep or small children, but plenty of fish and, above all, peace and the freedom to soar to the ceiling of the sky without falling prey to its only predator.

~

Donella's designer old lady trouser leg masks have not caught on, but I may have come up with a more lucrative money-making side-line.

Many people seem to think that anyone who writes books that are published will be on roughly the same level of salary as J K Rowling. This is very much not true. A relative handful will make big money, while the rest of us would probably be better off working part-time for B&Q. But I prefer wandering around Europe and eating and drinking, and am always on the lookout for a little additional income. Wherever we have lived I have tried to spot and climb through the window of opportunity. For some reason, I always pick the wrong window. In rural France my scheme for selling bottled water from our well was a non-starter as inordinate amounts of cow pats and chemical field dressings made it not only undrinkable but highly toxic. I could not interest a manufacturer in my inspired plan for a garlic car-freshener, and when I staged a boot sale in the field behind our water mill, mistranslation meant the vendors mostly turned up with old boots to sell.

But I reckon my latest wheeze could be a winner.

I got the idea from a friend who lives in a part of France, where the most severe category of lockdown is in place. Residents have to have a good reason for leaving their homes, and one of them is to walk a dog. My friend likes to get out and about and visit a lady friend for an evening apéritif, so takes a dog lead with him. If encountering any gendarmes on the lookout for lockdown-flouters, he will wave his lead and shout out for Gaston, his completely fictional French Bulldog.

Such has been the success of his ruse that he reckons a website selling imaginary dogs would be a real winner. Now that ownership has become such a trend, his customers would be able to own a dog without all the bother and cost of looking after a real one. For a relatively small donation, they would receive a full and impressive pedigree, a lead and bowl to leave in the kitchen when friends visited.

Refining his idea, I think a subscription scheme would be even more of a money-spinner. For a modest monthly amount, subscribers would receive imaginary packages of the best quality dog food and a newsletter containing tips and articles about looking after their non-existent dog. Given the soaring cost of vet's bills, I can't see how, unlike so many money-spinners I've tried, this scheme could fail.

~

The Isle of Wight is said to be the most haunted place in Britain, It's also claimed that conkers were invented here and that it's the sunshine capital of the UK. This indicates an active and imaginative Island marketing team, and I'm beginning to think that the presence of red squirrels on the Island is just another PR puff.

YouTube is bursting with video clips of grey squirrels performing acrobatic feats to the sound of Mission Impossible theme tune to break into apparently impregnable bird feeders. Despite a dozen hanging cages, bowls and trays of bird feed lining the fence on the other side of which are a thousand trees, we have yet to see a squirrel of any colour.

~

It may sound obvious, but the trick with visiting people who are old or very ill is to work out if they want a visit, or would rather you did not trouble them.

It's easy to feel a glow of self-righteousness and think you are doing your duty, but it may be only you that's getting pleasure from the visit. With our next door neighbours it's much simpler. If we are not welcome either the patient or his wife will tell us to bugger off.

Like a lot of people nearing the end of their lives, Jack likes to reminisce about his younger days. He particularly likes to talk about his favourite foods from those days, and wistfully recalls bowls of jellied eels and slabs of bread pudding. He could have them now, he says, but he knows they would not taste as they did in his youth.

Since we arrived we have been promising each other a visit to the local Conservative Club, but it has not happened. He said the other day that he used to like a Bloody Mary, and we have arranged to call in on Christmas Day morning with a bottle of vodka and a carton of tomato juice. I just hope he will still be with us to drink a toast to the coming year. Before we left and Mary was showing Donella her garden, I said that he was very brave.

He asked me what I meant and I said how much I admired how he kept going.

Shaking his head and speaking slowly as if to an

idiot, he said: 'Not a lot of choice is there?'

When I hear young people whining about how awful their lives are, I wish I could be around when they are old and infirm and know the awful truth.

~

More worrying news about the sanctity of our situation.

Before starting negotiations to buy Greenbanks we checked the ten acres of deciduous trees were part of the country park and so immune from the avaricious advances of property developers. Now it seems our information was wrong. According to the nice lady at the Golden Hill Country Park office, the woodland is not under their management, and worse, it does not belong to the Council and is in private hands.

Donella has booked an appointment with the Tree Protection Officer at Newport, and we must wait until next week to find out if we could end up with a building plot where the giant oaks overhang our peaceful garden.

∞∞∞∞

6

"Although the Island is famous for its sandy beaches, holiday camps and music festivals, it has gained a reputation amongst writers as 'Britain's Magical Island' because of its long history of paranormal events which include ghostly encounters, time-slips, occult practices and its legendary association with the mysterious Druids"

Gary Biltcliff, writing in the Fountain International Magazine

Early morning mists have stolen the monument on Tennyson Down, and wind, rain and cold are the default weather settings.

The roof of our summerhouse is still a frosty white most mornings, the tracks and pathways through the country park remain sticky and uncertain, but the auguries of a change of seasons are on the wing.

This morning two blue tits arrived at the nesting box on the garden shed and seemed to be intent on a set-to. At first I thought they were disputing territorial rights, but then saw the smaller one slip through the hole as the other flew back and forward, beak filled with nesting material.

To mark the occasion, I have taken the crampons off my walking boots. I've haven't slipped and fallen for at least a week, and don't want to look like I am heading for the north face of K2 when passing old ladies in bedroom slippers taking their dogs for the daily walk.

As I passed the fort this afternoon, an old dog came limping towards me. Its haunches were close to the ground and it was obviously struggling to stay upright. Its condition seemed more poignant because it was a big and obviously once powerful German Shepherd. As we approached it looked at me with a bemused and somehow entreating look as if I might be able to explain why it was no longer able to run free and fast or even move without pain. I patted its head as its owner appeared and I saw she was on crutches. Her old dog was slow but she was even slower.

As she drew nearer, I saw her as she must have looked a half century before. She had a page boy haircut and her face was ravaged by life and time, but the young version showed fleetingly as she looked at the dog. I asked the age of the dog and she said he was twelve. Although that is near the limit for an Alsatian and the loss of the back legs showed the beginning of the end, I said she would have the pleasure of his company for a good few years yet.

She smiled sadly and nodded as if she knew why I had said what I said, then replied: 'I don't think so, but it would be nice if he could see me out…'

She hobbled off and the dog looked at me and then her, then limped off. I watched them go and thought how unfair it is that, just as we learn to appreciate the simple things in life, we grow too old to enjoy them.

~

I don't have the figures to hand, but I wouldn't mind a small punt that the ratio of Islanders who have a dog in their lives is far higher than the national average. Apart from the rural surroundings, the higher widow/widower density might be a cause or effect. Widows are much more common than widowers and many of them replace a dead husband with a dog. Some of those I talk to believe they have got a better deal now. As one clearly merry widow said to me the other day, her labradoodle gives her unconditional love, doesn't make carnal demands nor leave smelly socks and underpants lying around. He farts, but somehow it doesn't smell as foul as her husband's. Best of all, Biggles never tells her what to do or how to think. He may pee on the floor occasionally, but never leaves the toilet seat up.

On the other hand and whatever they say, I reckon a number of woman who claim to cherish their new independence must miss being told what to do. A middle-aged woman who stopped for a chat the other day told me she had divorced her husband because of his controlling behaviour, then hurried off obediently when her yappy little dog snapped at her heels. Another said it was the third time her terrier had insisted on climbing the slope up to the fort that day and looked blankly at me when I suggested she could have said no.

~

Our daily visit next door. Mary sits at her latest thousand-piece jigsaw, concentrating with a frown on one corner of the sky over the Rialto Bridge. She is getting through at least one puzzle a week, yet clearly takes no pleasure from them. I suppose it is an attempt to take her mind away from what she knows is coming.

Jack sits in his usual chair, which seems to be getting bigger as he grows ever slighter. His skin looks almost transparent, and I get a sudden image of him fading away till he disappears completely. It might not be a bad way to go.

We talk in desultory terms about the past and times and people long gone. Now and then, Mary looks up and at him and seems about to say something. Then she shakes her head and returns to picture-postcard Venice.

I can't imagine what it would be like to know that I would soon be losing Donella. Jack and Mary are guilty of no more than growing old together, and there seems no sense or justice in tearing them apart.

Today I will be treading on a serpent's tail and must take care not to disturb the sleeping beast.

It is not a real serpent, but the name the ancients gave the unusual snaking trail of sedentary rock that makes up the spine of the Island. It is in a combination which is of interest to geologists and occultists alike. The geologists because of the unusual nature of the formation; the occultists because they believe it is a magic leyline.

Some of the almost vertical layers were formed by the awesome pressures that created the European Alps. The main element is greensand, an iron-bearing, hard sandstone known in ancient times as 'firestone'.

A rare strata forms what at a fair stretch of the imagination could be the shape of a monstrous dragon or serpent's tail snaking across the Island from the Needles in the west to Brading in the east. How the Ancients knew that something special lay beneath their feet and what course it took we cannot know, but it gives some credence to the occultists' belief.

For sure, the serpent's tail passes through a wealth of mystical and allegedly supernatural sites, from prehistoric burial mounds, giant standing stones said to have powers to raise the dead and ends at a sacred grove near Brading. On the way there's even a long-gone manor house which renews itself complete with party-goers every New Year's Eve.

Whatever you think of the tales of myth and magic surrounding this part of the Island, to be alone and walking the serpent's tail when the wind soughs and dusk falls can be a spine-tingling experience for anyone with a sense of time and place and history.

~

Every day is a good day for walking the downs, but today the sun shines and my spirits are high. I hope my pleasure at what is to come is not sweetened by the fact that I will be walking free as air, while just a handful of miles across the Solent, others have to huddle at home under strict lockdown rules. The moment of *schadenfreude* gives me a twinge of guilt, but I must admit it is not much of a twinge.

My ramble starts prosaically enough through the golf course overlooking Freshwater Bay. Unlike many golf clubs, this one welcomes walkers who stick to the footpath and won't whinge if hit by a misdirected ball.

I meet a healthy selection of walkers, all clearly glad to be out and about on a glorious day with a panoramic view across fields, rolling downlands and to the greeny-grey sea. I get an almost hundred percent response to my greetings, and the only blank comes from a small man wearing a large pair of earphones and clearly conducting the orchestra he is listening to. An earnest lady of my age overtakes, pushing herself along with two hiking poles. To me the new fashion looks as if the users have left skis behind and not noticed, but I'm told the sticks help with purchase, posture and gait.

Families and couples with or without dogs smile and nod as we pass, and I stop for a chat with a man on an off-road mobility scooter. He has a big, young and eager dog on a long lead, and when it gets excited and tears off it appears to be towing him in its wake. I often see him trundling down the track by the Yar, and he is obviously not going to let the absence of legs stop him from enjoying the open air. When I thought I knew him well enough to ask how he had lost his legs, he smiled resignedly over my shoulder at a long-ago memory and said: 'Pure carelessness.'

The Village of Brook

'Being a 12-year-old on a bike on the Isle of Wight with my brother and sister and ma and pa is for me the epitome of happiness. We didn't stay on the chic side of the island, but near brook beach, where there's black sand.'

Handbag designer and breathy star of sexy 1960's pop hit *Je t'aime moi non plus* Jane Birkin on her childhood on the Isle of Wight

∞∞∞∞

The church at Brook

The nearest road is far away, and I am on my own but in good company with nature. It is a rare enough experience to be out of sight and sound of modern times anywhere in overstuffed Britain; here on the high downs with distant views of where a glittering sea meets the great dome of the blue sky, it's especially rewarding. It is also a nostalgic journey, as this part of the Island and I go back a long way together.

Although it appears to be largely unchanged, the village of Brook was once home mainly to people who helped work the land. Now it smells of money and you rarely see a sign of life at the end of long drives to cottages which have become mini-mansions. The quietitude may be because the owners are to be found at even more expensive homes on the mainland, or prefer to stay in when the common people are about.

Apart from property embellishments and breath-taking prices and the average income of the residents, little seems to have changed since I first came here to camp in the fields between the village and the cliffs. The Hanover Stores has transmogrified into a characterful home that never was, but the aroma of ham, cheese, chocolate and animal feed stays with me. So does sitting in the gardens with tea and cake when my mother made the expedition from Portsmouth just to see that I was being fed properly.

Small boys either like camping or decidedly not. I loved it and joined the cubs, sea scouts and Royal Marine cadets at the same just to go camping on the Island. I wasn't worried about weaving my woggles or learning to tie a Turk's Head or knock out *A Life on the Ocean Waves* on my fife; the appeal was being under canvas as much as possible through the summer months. Perhaps the appeal of seemingly limitless space and the eternal renewing of nature was because I was brought up in the most populous city in the land, where our playgrounds were the bombsites resulting from the Portsmouth Blitz. For whatever reason, I lived for my summer camps on the mysterious and distant Isle of Wight. I loved the long days of going pretending to be lost in the wilderness with only a sausage sandwich and a bottle of home-made lemonade to keep me alive. I loved not washing except in the sea and sleeping on the ground safe from the rain pattering on the canvas roof. I loved the treasure hunts, the midnight walks and the chance to poison unloved teachers or senior figures when on the cooking roster. Depending on behaviour, boys would be detailed for latrine digging or cooking duties. I was often on both in the same day.

One of my gang's regular excursions would be to climb the hill to a series of ancient burial mounds and the grand Brook House. Said to be the highest property on the Island, it was at that time the home of J.B. Priestley, and he had a very fine apple orchard.

The wildly successful author of *The Good Companions* and *An Inspector Calls* was notoriously grumpy and known ironically to his friends as Jolly Jack. But he was an affable host and eminent visitors to Brook House included historian AJP Taylor (who lived at Yarmouth) actors Michael Denison and Dulcie Gray and poet Louis McNeice.

On one scrumping mission we were shouted at and pursued by a stout man in collarless shirt and braces. We easily outdistanced him and it was probably only the gardener, but I like to think we were chased by the great JB himself.

~

The Isle of Wight summer camps really were the happiest of days and times.

Each day there would be organised activities to teach us how to start a fire with a pair of spectacles and how to climb or fall down cliffs, but best of all were the manhunts. We would wait impatiently as a teacher loped off in plimsolls, baggy shorts and jungle hat, then pursue him across fields and through forests and over streams until arriving safely back at camp or being caught by a whooping band of small savages. Our faces would be blackened and the tips of our spears hardened in the fire, and the more unpopular the master, the sweeter the prize if we ran him down to ground, tied him to a tree and pretended to run him through.

Not quite Lord of the Flies, but close.

~

I'm sitting in a sheep-filled field, eating lunch and admiring the distant glitter of the choppy sea with the wavelets reflecting the sun like a million shattered looking-glass fragments. Nearer to, the dazzling white of lofty cliffs and then the lush emerald green of downland grass. It seems a very long way from the pandemic.

Rock of Ages: The ancient standing stone at Mottistone

As Egypt's Old Kingdom drew to a close and a couple of millennia before the first bucket and spade holidaymakers arrived, the Beaker people made their home on the Isle of Wight.

Over the millennia they had made the journey from their origins in Central Europe, and called their new home 'Whit' or 'What rises above the sea'.

They fought and lived off the land with Bronze Age weapons and tools, and buried their dead under large, circular mounds of earth. More than three hundred barrows or tumuli have been found and excavated around the Island, unearthing human remains, precious possessions, weapons and the distinctive and much-prized pottery for which the race is named.

Five barrows lie on this part of the Island's spine, though we cannot know if they were made here because of the magical significance of the leyline, or just because they liked to bury their dead in high places.

Standing in what is now no more than a grassy knoll, I try to imagine what it must have been like to live in those perilous times. While I'm here, I also take a moment to harness the power of the firestone beneath my feet to help me pick the winning EuroMillions numbers for this weekend. After my wish, I uncross my fingers and look up at the megalith which pre-dates the barrows by at least a thousand years.

The Longstone at Mottistone is four metres high and beside it lies a smaller horizontal slab, also made from magical firestone. They are part of what the experts call a long barrow, which is a burial tradition going back six thousand years and where bodies were laid out in lines to be fed upon by birds and beasts.

According to legend, the giant rock was thrown from St Catherine's Point ten miles distant as part of a wager with the Devil. His smaller stone landed short and so he lost the bet, though we do not know what was at stake.

We do know that the site lies east to west and could be part of the rituals of sun worship as it was then thought the sun's rays had the power to summon the spirits of the dead. In later times, the Saxons named it the 'Moot' or meeting stone, where tribes would gather to settle their differences with words rather than blows.

~

One of the things I like most about the Island is the way it's not too savvy about marketing its little-known treasures. A good example comes in the shape of a horse which became a star of stage and screen.

An ancestor of our current MP was Lord of the Manor at Mottistone. A friend of Churchill, General Jack Seely first led his horse Warrior into battle in 1914. Eight million horses did not survive the Great War, but Warrior became known as The Horse The Germans Could Not Kill. Back home on the Island he lived till the grand old age of 33, and a hundred years after his exploits, he was awarded the animal equivalent of the Victoria Cross. Because of the film and stage play, the whole world now knows about Warrior, if not where he came from.

~

Unlike Ancient Rome, all roads on the Isle of Wight do not lead to Newport. It just seems that way.

I reckon if you stood on the flyover long enough you would see every car and motorbike on the Island whizzing, pootling or grumbling by, including a fair number of agricultural vehicles.

The roads leading to and ensnaring the Island's county town are always busy, and this is because nearly all the sort of places you need to make a trip to at some time are to be found here. If you need to complain about your Council Tax, get a broken limb seen to, shop at Lidl prices, buy a lawn mower or visit a relative behind bars, you will need to visit Newport or its environs.

Home to 25,000 and bested in numbers only by Ryde, the town probably started life as a Roman settlement, though appears to have been ignored by Saxons and Jutes. The 'new port' was granted a charter in the late 12th century and soon took over from Newtown as the premier trading port. Despite its lack of flavour-of-the-moment outlets, we find you can get pretty much what you want at Newport. That was also the conclusion of a Tripadvisor-type reviewer in 1794, who said it was a 'well-built, handsome town, the shops numerous and as superbly stocked as in most of the English cities.' Note that he did not say 'other' English cities so the idea of the Island as a place apart was already taking hold.

I suppose because you don't expect to encounter them at any distance from the sea, I find inland ports particularly beguiling, and Newport's is a real beauty. Unlike our home town of Portsmouth and not having had any visitations from the Luftwaffe or modernist architectural vandals trying to make a name for themselves, the centre is pretty constant, undamaged and awash with often striking examples of fine buildings of Medieval, Regency and Victorian vintage.

Of particular note are the Guildhall and Institute, both examples of the work of prominent eighteenth-century architect John Nash. Amongst many celebrated projects, he converted Buckingham House into a palace for his friend and patron George IV, designed much of London's Regent Street and worked on the Royal Pavilion at Brighton. He retired to the Isle of Wight having achieved fame if not fortune, and died penniless at East Cowes in 1835. The final humiliation came when his coffin was taken to the church at dead of night to prevent his creditors from claiming his corpse.

It's undeniable that the High Street has seen better days, but the shopping centre still bustles and the people using it generally seem happy to be there. There's a traffic-free and spacious square dominated by the Minster church, which is dedicated to Thomas Becket and contains some interesting stuff. Newport even has its own Harry Potter-esque Diagon Alley.

Leaving the square, we pass two scruffy blokes sitting on a bench outside the minster. They are both toying with roll-up prison slim fags and cans of heavy-duty lager. At their feet are rolled-up sleeping bags, some overstuffed carrier bags and a large plastic bottle of industrial strength lager. One of the men has an upside-down ball cap next to him on the bench and I think about chucking a pound coin in it till my wife sees me reaching for a pocket and gives me a stern nudge. It's not that she objects to me donating to the homeless, but is reminding me of a time in Normandy when I was mistaken for a beggar rather than just a very untidy dresser. It was a hot day and I had sat down outside a posh hotel in Normandy and taken my beret off to mop my brow. Within minutes, a grand lady with a tiny dog on a lead had swished down the steps, fumbled in her purse and tossed a handful of coins into my hat. I was all for staying there and seeing how much we could collect, but my wife moved us on.

As we left the two men behind, she said they looked too smart to be homeless men, but then she was comparing them with me. I said I thought they might be actors, employed by the council to show visitors that Newport was not behind the times.

Newport Rowing Club

'Boaty businesses' at Newport

The Medina estuary starts at the heart of the town and runs past thoughtfully updated or carefully dishevelled warehouses and boaty businesses for the seventeen kilometres to the top of the estuary at Cowes. On the way are a couple of upmarket marinas and, much more interestingly for me, a number of mud-choked creeks and inlets filled with dodgy-looking jetties and even dodgier-looking old boats. In some fields there are grime-encrusted caravans which were getting on a bit when paddle steamers were plying their trade in the Solent.

We're sitting alongside the jetty, throwing bread at the gulls, ducks and swans and reviewing the outcome of our visit to the Tree Preservation Man. It's fair to say that we are in general relieved, with, as lately seems inevitable, some reservations.

A tall, enthusiastic and almost tree-like man, he showed us lots of plans and documents and explained that, with one exception, he had slapped a TPO (Tree Preservation Order) on the whole ten acres of the privately owned woodland on the other side of our fence. That means nobody can cut them down or interfere with them in any way without facing a very heavy fine. That was also why he had left an unprotected strip of several metres directly alongside our fence, so the owner could manage the dozen or so oaks and lop off any branches overhanging our garden.

'But what if he decides to cut those trees down and apply for permission to build a very thin and long house next to our fence?' asked my wife.

'I suppose he could apply,' said the tree man with a lazy smile, 'but it would, as you say, have to be very narrow and I think it highly unlikely he would get permission for a house there, especially one with no approach road except for the bridle path. And it would have to go through the badgers' sett, and we wouldn't want them to have to re-locate would we?'

'No,' said I with feeling, 'and especially not to our back garden.'

∞∞∞∞ .

Haunted Houses and Ghostly Goings-On

The Isle of Wight is said to be the most haunted place in Great Britain, though there seems to be no official league table. The long list of allegedly spook-ridden places includes:

The 9th-century **Arreton Manor,** which is allegedly haunted by the shade of Elizabethan Annabelle Leigh, thrown from an upper window by her older brother after she saw him murder their father to gain his inheritance. Now the small figure in a blue dress walks the passageways and climbs the stairs for all eternity, doomed to endlessly re-enact her sudden demise. She has been seen by staff and visitors, and the room from where she suffered defenestration is said to be cold in the hottest of summers.

All that remains of **Knighton Gorges Manor** are the pillars at the gateway, but there is a plethora of ghostly goings-on in and around the premises. The great house itself is said to appear on New Year's Eve, and party-going spectres include an 18th-century MP who committed suicide there after suffering disastrous gambling losses. His ghost is also said to roam the grounds on a spectral horse on the anniversary of his death.

Appuldurcombe House is an imposing manor house at Wroxall, but lies in ruin behind its carefully-restored frontage. It was mostly destroyed by a stray bomb in World War II, and is said to abound with sightings of ghostly monks, spectral carriages, strange lights and inexplicable drops in temperature.

Also at Wroxall, **The Star Inn** is a recently-declared favourite local for spooks and accompanying spectral events. It started when a security camera captured a glass falling unaided from a table in the empty public bar, and supernatural events are said to occur regularly.

In 1737, a woodcutter named Michael Morey was executed for killing his grandson. His body was left to rot on the gibbet, which is now to be found on show at the **Hare & Hound** pub near the county town of Newport. It is said that a shadowy figure wielding a chopper can often be seen in the vicinity, though whether it is the shade of the hanged man or a modern-day member of a stag party is not known.

Before becoming a major tourist attraction, **The Ventnor Botanical Gardens** was the setting for a hospital specialising in tuberculosis cases. To this day, ghostly doctors, nurses and patients are seen almost as frequently as the paying customers.

Just up the track from where we live and built during the Napoleonic era, **Golden Hill Fort** at Freshwater is now a collection of swish houses and apartments. But, on certain nights, it is said that a general murdered by his men can be seen walking woefully along the ramparts. His presence is also registered by the smell of his favourite pipe tobacco.

Another popular venue for ghostly goings-on is **Carisbrooke Castle**. Though at one time a temporary prison for the doomed Charles I, there are no claims for manifestations of his astral presence. Regular spectres include a woman who drowned in the well (her face can be seen in the water at regular intervals) and an other-worldly man, woman and their pack of dogs circling the premises.

Now converted to upmarket apartments, the former **Whitecroft Hospital** at Gatcombe was once an asylum. Nowadays, as well as current residents, former patients and doctors and nurses can be seen flitting around the grounds.
Near Chillerton, **Billingham Manor** is said to be haunted by the traditional Grey Lady and also a long-dead man in red.

Even **Sandown Pier** likes to get in on the act since a ghostly figure walked through the stage curtains after an evening performance. Many other sightings have been reported by visitors, whether all sober or not is not known.

Even the Poet Laureate's home **Farringford** at Freshwater gets into the spectral hit parade with claims that the great man has been seen taking his ease and enjoying his pipe in the grounds. His wife Emily is also said to appear while attending to the gardens, and the inevitable phantom carriage is said to rattle along the driveway at certain times.

NB. *It is not known if the fact that most of the premises above are open to and in search of visitors has any bearing on the veracity of the ghostly tales surrounding them.*

7

"Listening now to the tide in its broad-flung shipwrecking roar,
Now to the scream of a maddened beach dragged by the wave."

From *Maud*, by Alfred Lord Tennyson

Had we lived in the same time frame, Alfred Lord Tennyson would have been a distant neighbour, and we might well have met while shopping.

In contention for the title of most popular poet of the Victorian era, Tennyson lived for close on forty years in Farringford, a grand Neo-Gothic house sitting below the rolling downland named in his honour. It is a curiosity that in southern England 'downs' invariably occupy lofty positions, and a monument to the author on his favourite dog-walking route marks the highest point in West Wight.

Tennyson and his wife Emily had been on the look-out for a long-term home since their marriage in 1850. Because of his enthusiasm for the poetry of Keats, he decided to look around the Island in which the leader of the Romanticism Movement had chosen to work. Alfred obviously liked what he saw, and he and an expectant Emily moved into Farringford with their little son Hallam in 1856. The couple lived there for the rest of their lives. Prince Albert's favourite poet loved to walk the downs above the house every day, thought the air, as he was wont to say, worth at least sixpence a pint. With him on his daily walk would be either his Siberian Wolfhound Karenina or Afghan sheepdog.

Pestered by fans who would dog his walks and gather at the gates, Tennyson and his family moved to the mainland each summer from 1869, but always returned to the place and home they loved.

After his death, the grand house remained in the family until 1945 then became an hotel. We stayed there for a wedding anniversary in the 1970s when it was owned and operated by the holiday camp legend, Fred Pontin.

Nowadays and after millions of pounds of private investment, Farringford House is a museum dedicated to the People's Poet.

Rare is the week when I do not follow in Tennyson's

footsteps.

It's a bracing experience in any weather, especially when the wind blusters and you can hear the 'shipwrecking roar of the wave-maddened beach far below' (© A. Tennyson).

My usual starting point is an old chalk quarry just up the road from the excellent Highdown Inn. From the quarry there's a choice between a gently rising track or a sometimes-vertiginous set of wooden stairs. The track leads to Nodes Beacon, a half-sized replica of an ancient warning of invasion and sea mark for sailors. The stairway leads to Tennyson's Cross, which replaced the beacon in 1895.

Walkers are very much spoiled for choice in this part of the Island, and I could take any one of a dozen paths and hike for more than twenty miles without troubling a road. Today I shall head west across the top of the down to The Needles lighthouse and Napoleonic Battery, then down to Alum Bay and across country to home.

Ahead, a small group of steers amble on and off the track and regard me incuriously as I pass. They are used to people, which is just as well as it is unthinkable what might happen if they were spooked into a mini-stampede. The cliff edge looms close, and considering the absence of any fencing their casual wandering poses an intriguing mystery. How is it they know not to get too close to the cliff edge and deadly drop to the beach? Even some humans get too close and pay the price. I regularly pass cowpats mere feet from the edge of the abyss, yet the incidence of flying cows is extremely rare.

In 2008, a lady was sunbathing on the beach near

Tennyson Downs and decided to have a dip. Within seconds of her starting down to the water, a cow landed on the exact spot where she had been lying. A coincidence of the type beloved by journalists everywhere was that the lady was a resident of Cowes.

~

Up here, the view and prevailing south-westerly wind are equally breath-taking.

On one side of the narrowing peninsula lies the unbroken sea with its constantly shifting and shimmering patterns and colours. They range from stormy steel-grey to azure blue and emerald green when the sun shines and the tide is right. Round the corner lie the multi-coloured cliff faces of Alum Bay and the distant landmarks of the Hampshire and Dorset coast. On a good day one can see the Isle of Purbeck and its Old Harry Rocks. Dead ahead are the Needles rocks and lighthouse, and a Victorian defence system that, unlike the so-called Palmerston's follies, actually engaged an enemy.

∞∞∞∞

In a survey of Tripadvisor reviews, The Needles was voted the 10th most beautiful walk in the United Kingdom. With competition like Arthur's Seat in Edinburgh, The Lizard in Cornwall and The Giant' Causeway in County Antrim, I reckon that's not a bad result.

I don't know who decided the chain of rocks lying off the westernmost point of the Island should be called The Needles. To me they look more like the poorly maintained teeth in a giant's lower jaw.

According to the guide books, they suited the name more when two of them tapered to narrow points. The tallest was 120 feet above the sea, and called Lot's Wife. Though made of chalk rather than salt, Lot's Wife and her companion rock took a spectacular tumble into the water in 1764.

Work on the lighthouse began in the 1850s, so it's a safe bet that the Poet Laureate would have stood at the same vantage point as me and watched the progress.

I'm looking along the barrel of a massive cannon which appears to be pointing at the mainland. In fact, it and its fellows were put in place to protect the south coast from unwelcome attention.

Alongside the Needles, work on the Old Battery began in 1861 and by 1893 the state-of the-art-ofwarfare muzzle-loading cannons took a team of nine men to load, run out and fire. The projectiles weighed 256 lbs (116 kilo) but never flew in anger. The guns remained in place until 1903, when they were disposed of by simply chucking them into the sea. Two were recovered and remind visitors of how much more efficient we have become at killing people in a little more than a century.

Sited nearby, the New Battery had even bigger and better cannons, and they saw brief action in WWII when some German Motor Torpedo Boats attempted a night landing.

Both batteries were de-activated after the War, but the site was used for experiments on Blue Streak and other missiles in the early 1950s.

~

For children born soon after World War II, no visit to the Isle of Wight was complete without a trip to see the multi-coloured cliff faces at Alum Bay. Technically speaking, the colours come from oxidised iron compounds, but to us they were a mystical wonder.

We didn't know or care that Italian inventor Guglielmo Marconi had successfully sent wireless communications two thousand miles across the Atlantic from the bay in 1903 and set the scene for global communications. We were there to queue up to buy a test tube and be let loose on the coloured sands to fill it. Clearly, we were much easier to please in those sometimes grey and always simpler days.

Where Marconi's genius was put into play is now an amusement park where you can buy sand-filled glass gee-gaws, locally-made sweets, have a meal or take a ride on a chair lift to the beach below for a boat trip around the Needles.

Apart from the updating, Alum, Bay hasn't changed that much since my childhood, and is always busy in the summer months. Perhaps it shows how simple and even old-fashioned entertainments can still appeal to today's youngsters. Or perhaps it shows that the sort of children who come to the Isle of Wight for a holiday are not the same as those whose parents take them to Orlando Disneyland.

Alum Bay from the Needles Battery

On the way back past the quarry and along the woodland trails behind his home, I stop off at Tennyson's corner shop.

Just up the road from a rare thatched church and across from the old gates to Farringford, Orchard Brothers' Grocery Store has been in the same family hands for more than 150 years. I occasionally call in, and it's nice to know I am standing where the Poet Laureate would pop in to pick up a plug of his favourite brand of baccy.

~

'The railway did not go further than Brockenhurst, and the steamer, when there was one, from Lymington felt itself in no way bound to wait for the omnibus which brought as many of the passengers as it could from the train. We crossed in a rowing boat. It was a still November evening. One dark heron flew over the Solent backed by a daffodil sky. Next day we went to Farringford and looking from the drawing-room window I thought "I must have that view," and I said so to him when alone. Tennyson himself said 'we will go no further; this must be our home.'

From Lady Emily Tennyson's diary on the 10th November 1853. The next day Tennyson arranged to lease Farringford for £2 a week with an option to buy. Three years later his earnings were £2000 a year, and he agreed to buy Farringford and its grounds and farm and parkland for £6,900. Works written on the Island include The *Charge of the Light Brigade* and *Maud*, and *Crossing the Bar* was composed on a trip across the Solent to the mainland.

After sharing his favourite walk and corner shop, I'm stopping off to pay my respects to Tennyson's wife.

At the end of what was then an exceptionally long life he was laid to rest in 1892 near Robert Browning in Poet's Corner at Westminster Abbey. Emily lived on only four years more, and lies in the cemetery at All Saints Church. It is on my way from Greenbanks to a favourite riverside walk, and I often take a seat near Emily's altar tomb. Other members of the family are buried or have memorials nearby, including son Lionel who died and was buried at sea in 1886. This has been a holy place for a long time, starting with a wooden church in the 9th century. The remnants of the first Saxon stone church are still to be seen.

As a one-time gravedigger in Portsmouth, I know that all cemeteries seem peaceful even when traffic roars by. Far from any busy road, All Saints is especially serene. Another attractive feature is that the churchyard would almost qualify as an arboretum, with sometimes exotic trees brought from around the world by returning merchants. The mix of imposing and ornate memorials, simple stones and wooden crosses marks the different stations of the residents, but there are no social barriers as wealthy landowners lie alongside those who worked their land, and admirals next to common sailors and smugglers.

Sadly, even hallowed ground is no guarantee of undisturbed eternal rest when it comes to the whims of the sacred badger. A family recently set up home in an occupied corner, and the bodies were relocated like householders in the path of a high-speed train route.

Despite that, this is a splendid place for contemplation on life and, of course, death. Although my plan for when I leave the stage is to be reunited with my parents in a Portsmouth cemetery, I can see it would be pleasant to spend the rest of time looking over the river and the life in and around it.

Tennyson's Top Ten

In a survey (which probably means the surveyors made the results up) these are said to be Tennyson's most popular and must-read works:

In Memorium
Tithonus
The Lady of Shalott
Mariana
Crossing the Bar
The Charge of the Light Brigade
Break, Break, Break
The Morte d'Arthur
Ulysses
The Lotus Eaters

According to the local paper, the battle for the siting of the new primary school is becoming more than a little acrimonious.

Understandably, parents who live in Freshwater want the new school to be built on the site of the old one in their village. Parents who live in Yarmouth believe the money should be spent within their boundaries.

We may be biased, but the right decision seems a no-brainer. The school down the track from us has playing fields and is at least twice the size of the Yarmouth school, with easy access and lots of parking. Also, the majority of pupils live in Freshwater. The argument offered by Yarmouth parents seems to boil down to Freshwater being not as attractive as their town, nor anywhere near as sophisticated. It has got as far as a Yarmouthian former teacher describing our village as a 'cultural desert.' As we have a library, sports centre with swimming pool, a Poet Laureate's former home, a couple of museums, a library, book shop and any number of arts and crafts shop, I think that's a rather unfair comment.

Regardless of the pros and cons, there's to be an open meeting next month at our school where a representative of the County Council will be answering questions. I hope he brings a tin hat.

~

I've been doing my weekly sweep of the village charity shops. I am banned from going in any of them without my wife, but she will not know unless I buy something.

We don't need any more old ladies' trousers, apple

peeling and coring gadgets or singing salmon, but I can't resist doing the rounds just to see how much cheaper things can be than when they were new. My problem is buying things not because of need or even fancy, but on how much we would save on, say, a hand-wrought poker for the fire we don't have or a 3D viewer for the specially produced postcards we also don't have.

I arrived this morning to find I can cross one of my calls off the list. This will be good news for my wife and perhaps for local property prices. You can usually tell how badly or well a place is doing by the number of charity shops it can support. Before the PDSA called it a day, Freshwater had five. I take the closure as another sign of the upmarketing of the village, especially as the new occupants are selling what they call 'collectables.' It is interesting irony that the shop which sold things at a fraction of their original price has been taken over by a business which sells old things at more than they cost when new. It is also a sign that we are in the next phase of the gentrification/ trendification process which eventually benefits or, some might say, afflicts all villages.

There are still a handful of empty shops, the recently arrived vape centre has gone up in smoke, and it's telling that the newer businesses are of a certain genre. They include a craft shop with the usual off-the-wall name and featuring locally- created must-haves like hand-crafted overcoats for dogs and bath bombs (whatever they may be) which are kind to the planet. Across the road and near to a charity shop which looks in need of some charity and saying an 'upright' (respectable?) tanning studio is another new and exotically named outlet. Half of the shop front is taken up with what looks like the back end saying of a freight container. Looking closer I see that it a deliberate design feature and not the outcome of a driver ran out of road on the downhill bend. Above what's left of the window, a sign offers advice on unique lighting, hand-made jewellery and furniture made from driftwood.

Just up the road is another trendy outlet where you can choose from a selection of hand knitted beany and bobble hats each of which the proprietor promises is unique. Looking at the tag, I see that the price as well as the design is pretty unique.

The newest creatively named and priced outlet is housed in what looks like an old workshop, its yard strewn with items I first thought were waiting collection by a refuse truck. There are Belfast sinks, zinc baths and utility furniture that many a totter would have refused to take in my 1950s childhood. I recently stopped to check out the price tags and had to sit down on one of the rickety 'period' chairs.

Nowadays, 'old' means of little value, or sometimes when applied to people, worthless. Until recently, the use of 'vintage' was originally restricted to wine, cars and television comedy programmes. Now it can obviously be used to enhance the value of anything except old people. In the window, a battered and rusty pair of tins for kitchen storage are valued at £15 and any weavers and loom-owners in the village can snap up a vintage shuttle at a tenner a go. Of course, you can't blame the owners for taking advantage of current fads and getting what they can for their stock, and it's the customers who know something we don't and are shrewdly investing for the future price boom in battered buckets, or just have more money than sense.

Nostalgic as some of the items are, I think I will stick to The Alzheimer Society shop as my go-to outlet for a bedside table or set of spoons. Just as long as I can remember where it is, of course.

~

Having resisted the urge to buy a genuine vintage laminated 1950s kitchen table just like my mum used to use, I arrive home to find a small middle-aged man in our front garden. He is looking thoughtfully over the fence. I ask rather pointedly if I can help, and he introduces himself as the owner of the small woodland next door. I change my tone immediately, and offer him coffee and perhaps a coffee éclair in my most ingratiating manner. I was intent on enjoying the cake myself, but want to be at my most affable. This is partly because I have found in rural France it is always a good idea to keep on cordial terms with whoever owns the land on the other side of your fence, especially if it has lots of wood which burns well. Then there's the plot I have been hatching since learning that the trees nearest to our fence are not protected by a Protection Order. I don't really believe that the owner might seek planning permission to build a long and very thin cottage in the twelve feet of unprotected woodland beyond our fence. But it would be nice if we could buy it from him. That would mean we could manage the overhanging trees, put up a squirrel box and even a tree house for our youngest grandson to play in when he visits. Also, although I don't think the ten acres of protected woodland are likely to be given planning permission for a property development scheme in our lifetime, owning the unprotected tranche next to our fence would put my mind more at ease. From a more cynical perspective, it would also be what they call a ransom strip in the property business, and, despite my principles, I would be more than content to sell it off with the bungalow for a very inflated sum. The only entry and exit point for any development would be from the road directly outside out front door, and if that meant taking the money and buying a castle in France, I don't think my NIMBY concerns would last long.

~

Our visitor has departed, having enjoyed his coffee but leaving the éclair. This is some small consolation, as he was not the bearer of good news.

He seems a decent man, but made it clear he will not even consider selling us a metre of the land over our fence. In fact, he had come to tell us he intends cutting down the unprotected trees.

He has, he said, been having sleepless nights worrying about a fire starting accidentally or maliciously in his woodland and spreading to the trees and branches overhanging our fence, and from there to our home. As he points out, ours is the only house and garden with trees so close. And the forecast was for a dry and even arid summer.

Cutting down all the oaks in the unprotected zone might detract from the rustic appeal as seen from our garden or back windows, he said, but it would act as an effective firewall.

~

I have been on the phone to the structural surveyor who we consulted about the garage, and he seemed as worried as we are about the loss of the oaks across the fence. For him, though, it was for practical rather than aesthetic reasons.

As he said, trees the size of the dozen mature oaks drink a lot of water. If they were cut down, the thousands of gallons of rain and ditch water coming from the top of Golden Hill they would have lapped up would have to go somewhere. As our home was below the level of the line of trees, the new water course would inevitably find its way to our foundations. This would mean that as well as a shaky garage, we would have a shaky bungalow.

~

'The old place is looking good, eh?'

'Well, the garage is still there,' I grudgingly acknowledge say as we arrive home after a week, as we Islanders say, across the water with our family.

I wouldn't say so, but I'm not sure I'm actually pleased that the garage is still defying gravity. It's not that I'm looking forward to a fight with the insurance company, just that I don't like uncertainty. If the garage is going to go, better it go soon.

With summer approaching, I have to say Greenbanks is living up to its name. Due to our conservationist attitude towards mowing the lawn until it reaches knee-height, wild flowers and what other people might call weeds are springing up everywhere. The jasmine, honeysuckle, Virginia creeper and lavender bushes add a glorious splash of colour. Across the fence, the oak trees are in full leaf, and I am relieved to see that they are still there. The owner was not specific, but did say he would like to get the job done in the near future.

I park outside the garage and lug the cases into the sitting room. My wife puts the kettle on as I take my haversack and laptop to my study. It looks on to the road and is smaller than the average monk's cell, but it is a good place to hide while pretending to work. Donella has an office in the house and a studio in the summerhouse at the top of the back garden. I have the rest of the summerhouse to work in, and will take up residence with my PC when the full summer comes. It will be nice to work away from the house and easier to skive if my wife is not around. She is aware of the risk and has had venetian blinds fitted to all the windows so I will not be distracted by the view over the rooftops to Tennyson Down.

'Whatever's the matter?'

My wife is in the kitchen and can obviously hear me grunting as I wrestle with the door handle.

'I think the door's locked,' I say, before she reminds me that there is no lock on my study door.

Frowning, I lay my computer and haversack down and apply my shoulder to the door. It gives a little but refuses to open. I take a step back and in the manner of a TV cop, shoulder-charge the door. It flies open and my momentum carries me into the room before I stumble on something. I look down at it and then towards the ceiling. The long white thing on the carpet is a length of plaster coving. It has detached itself from where it masked the joint between wall and ceiling. Looking closer, I see that there is a distinct gap where a wall traditionally meets a ceiling. Further inspection shows that another length of coving is getting ready to measure its length on the floor, and there is worse. Eerily similar in shape if not yet size to the Nile Delta, a fissure has appeared at the top of the wall holding the window that overlooks the front garden. It runs down for about a metre, then disappears behind a framed painting of our old farmhouse in France. Quite sizeable lumps of plaster sit on my desk, and a fine powder covers the seat of my chair.

It has been the wettest winter and spring on record, and it seems that even the line of oak trees that the owner intends cutting down were not thirsty enough to stop our house heading down the slope to join our injured garage.

8

On a list in the *Independent* newspaper of the worst fifteen places to live in the United Kingdom, the Isle of Wight came in at number fifteen. The reasons given for the undesirableness of the Island was the high price of food and poor examination results. Those judged even more harshly included Blackpool, the entire counties of Somerset and Devon and the Gwent Valleys.

~

The sort-of good news is that the Crack of Doom has grown no wider.

Copying a wheeze from a James Bond film, I taped a length of my wife's hair across the narrowest point of the fissure running down my office wall. In a week the hair has not broken. This means that my wife has really strong and stretchy hair, or the house has stopped moving - at least for the moment.

Our surveyor has been round to take a look and confirmed it was indeed a crack in the plaster and that the wall behind it must have moved a bit. Apart from reminding us we had only paid for his cheapest walk-round-and-look-over option before buying Greenbanks, he recommended calling in a specialist structural expert. He would be able to tell us the cause of the movement and who if anyone we could sue. Except, of course, him.

After he left, we went to the pub to discuss our - and possibly the house's - next move. As my wife said, it was an irony how we had lived in any number of ancient properties abroad that had appeared to be on the point of collapse but had remained fairly intact. Now we were living in a modern one that might be on its way down the slope to join the collapsing garage.

My proposal after several glasses of Merlot that we set fire to the house, claim the insurance and do a runner to France was not given serious consideration. Nor was my idea that we should move into the summerhouse and let the bungalow out for a cheap rent with safety helmets supplied.

By closing time, we had explored all the options and decided to do no more than buy a proper crack meter and hope that our home has, like us, decided to go no more a-roaming.

Our neighbouring village of Norton Green is a place of two halves, and the off-road bit is exactly the sort of small community lots of people think they would like to retire to.

It's pretty without being quaint, and has bags of character. There's a nice mix of thatch and slate and stone and brick, and one of the cottages actually has roses rambling around the front door. The local pub has long gone and the only reminder of the old post office is the freshly painted red box set in a wall. But the integrity of the village/hamlet has not been violated by modern development. Things have changed a lot over the past hundred years, but Norton Green manages the trick of looking as if they haven't.

In times past, though, not everyone was a fan. The same 18th-century Tripadvisor-type reviewer who gave Newport a five-star rating thought that '…the little hamlet exhibits some rural cottages that have lately been erected, with more expense than taste.' Ouch.

One of those cottages has been home to a new friend and true caulkhead for more than half a century, and she has no plans for moving.

Sheila Hughes was born in a tiny terraced house in East Cowes in 1935. Her father was a boot and shoe repairer and maker in the days when footwear came very expensive and was mended rather than thrown away. He had a shop where he and brother Jack plied their trade, and Sheila remembers the visits to Osborne house to repair and supply officer's boots and belts.

Sheila went to school at Whippingham, near the church designed by Prince Albert. Attitudes had changed little since Victorian days, but despite the sometimes harsh discipline they were happy days for her. At home, bread and milk were delivered by horse and cart and the only car owner in the area was the butcher at the end of the road. Times were not easy but food was cheap and plentiful and vegetables came from the family allotment. She recalls that sometimes the officers would pay their bills with joints of meat mislaid from the kitchen.

Sheila moved on to the agricultural school at Freshwater and qualified as a herdswoman. She and her new husband bought the old cottage at Norton Green for £700. A widow for some years, her best friend and constant companion is Jill the collie. Their mutual adoration is obvious.

My father used to say that all you needed as a dog was to find a good owner. In that respect, Jill has hit the jackpot.

"I go to nature to be soothed and healed, and to have my senses put in order."

-John Burroughs, naturalist, essayist and poet
(1837-1921)

I feel rather than see or hear her, but know she is there.

In spite of the spines, the badgers obviously enjoy a hedgehog snack, but they don't have a taste for fox. Or perhaps they only go for the younger and more tender ones.

I have made almost friends with an elderly vixen, who comes to my call most nights. Her coat is drab and her teats sag and she has a bad leg, but she survives and has put on weight since I started feeding her. She won't yet take food from my hand, but will come close when nobody else is around.

I love to sit here with my fallen tree friend as night falls and wait for the old fox to appear. It is serenely peaceful and atmospheric and a good time and place for thinking thoughts beyond what I am having for supper. I used to think of these quiet times as truly communing with nature, but a poem by John Burroughs claims that it is with ourselves we are connecting at these times. Nature, he says, furnished the conditions and the solitude, and the soul furnishes the entertainment.

All in all, I can't see how I can argue with that.

~

Gathered outside the lych-gate, a group of parishioners stand talking. Some of the women look wistfully at the entrance to the church. The great doors are left unlocked during normal times, but fear of spreading the disease and infecting elderly worshippers mean services have been suspended and the doors locked. I notice that some of the men are looking wistfully at the nearby pub.

The lane twists down past a field of horses and a

ruined barn and then the river comes into sight. A World War II pill-box marks the start of the Causeway bridge across the Yar, and in a village-y sort of gesture, people often leave small unwanted items on the ledge of the slit overlooking the river. Sometimes it's bags of stale bread to feed the swans and ducks. Last week four trendy coffee cups and a biography of Elton John were on display. I see that the cups have gone but the Elton John book is still there, which may or may not be an indicator of local reading tastes.

The Causeway spans the Yar at a point just before the stream blossoms into the creek which winds its way to Yarmouth. The Causeway is actually more of a low bridge, built in the 17th century from a dam wall serving an old tidal mill which had stood there for three hundred years.

There's a small but enthusiastic gathering on the crest of the bridge, taking photos of or throwing bread at what must be some of the best-fed swans and ducks in the land. More than twenty mute swans see the advantages of living here, and I stop to talk to their unofficial guardians. Jenny looks up and smiles as she empties a large bag of sliced bread over the parapet. Sniffy people say that bread is not good for swans or ducks, but I don't think anyone has told the birds. Jenny and her husband Roger are a pleasant couple who monitor and record births and deaths and even rescue injured swans, once taking the patient to the animal hospital in the back of their Volvo estate.

Looking over the parapet I see what is causing the increased interest amongst the scrimmage of photographers. Some are using their phone cameras, but there's a sizeable proportion of tooled-up specialists. Invariably men of middle age and beyond, their dress code is a vaguely military and archaeological combination of Indiana Jones-style fedora hats or ear-enveloping beanies, many-pocketed body warmers, cargo trousers and business-like boots. The pockets are for any number of lenses and accessories, and they carry their wincingly expensive cameras attached to poles which rest on their shoulders as they march along the riverbank like patrolling pikemen.

They are in such number as there is a large, black bird jostling for attention amidst the whiteness, which is, quite interestingly, a collective noun for a gathering of swans. He or she is one half of a couple which appeared last month and stayed for a few days.

Black swans are native to Australia and there are thought to be no more than a hundred pairs in Britain. This one has obviously lost or split up with its mate, and returned alone. It seems quite at home and Jenny tells me she has been accepted by the others. She adds that it has been known for the two varieties of mute swans to mate, in which case their progeny will be known as blutes. I think about asking her what shade or colour the children of such a mixed union might be, but don't want to be thought of as racist so say goodbye and move on.

This small but special corner of what is known as the back of the Wight is one of five on the Island named as an Official Area of Outstanding Natural Beauty. Our OAONB also has the honour of being designated as a Site of Special Scientific Interest. I don't know about the science, but guess the beauty award comes from the enchanting combination of saltmarsh reed beds, sandbanks, mudflats, ancient water mills and thatched cottages. The place changes like and with the weather, which suits my restless eye. With copses and shorelines to explore and the sea a stroll away, it is one of my favourite places on the Island, or anywhere else.

A former railway worker's cottage stands at the end of the Causeway bridge, beside the track where the line ran alongside the river from Freshwater to Yarmouth. The service was started in 1889 to connect the thinly-populated west of the Island with Newport. It was never commercially successful and closed in 1953. Nowadays it is highly successful as a shared foot and cycle path, and no matter how busy the track, the walkers and joggers and cyclists rub along well. Except when the thankfully rare arse-in-the-air lycra lout races by.

As I pass the picket fence, an elderly man in the garden looks up from where he is struggling with a wheelie-bin full of cuttings. He rests against the bin and waves and smiles and I return the gesture.

John and Eileen moved into the cottage more than twenty years ago, and must get fed up with the number of people passing every day who tell them how lucky they are to live there. John was one of the thousands of children who contracted polio in the 1950s, but never complains about the horrors he must have gone through after waking up one morning to find himself partly paralysed. He has a sardonic sense of humour, and when I tried to sympathise with him when we first met, he smiled and said having one crippled leg was still preferable to having just one.

~

The riverside walk is part of a trail named in honour of a local equivalent of Leonardo da Vinci.

Born in 1635, Robert Hooke was a scientist, architect and polymath. He obviously liked to keep busy, and apart from inventing a special telescope to observe the planets, he studied microscopic organisms and in his spare time made architectural surveys on half the buildings destroyed in the great Fire of London.

For the next ten minutes I am kept busy exchanging nods, smiles or pleasantries with a procession of walkers, cyclists and joggers and the response rate is fourteen cordial replies and one grunt out of fifteen.

Over the years I have made informal studies and even kept a record of how or if strangers acknowledge my existence. It is interesting how the rate varies depending on location and population density.

In general, the rule is that the least populated and more rural, the higher the response rating. Walking in the Balkans I find it is invariably a hundred percent, but that is because four encounters is a busy day, and a friendly greeting is a way of showing you are not a bandit or serial killer in search of the next victim. In France, the response rate can actually exceed a hundred percent, as a simple '*Il faite beau, whey?*' ('nice weather, eh?) can result in a ten-minute conversation, with meeting and leaving handshakes and kisses on both cheeks. And all that from people you've never seen before.

I suppose averting one's eyes and pretending that someone is not there is understandable when you're in a high-crime area and meet someone who is looking for any excuse to start a fight or steal your phone and credit cards. In my home city of Portsmouth, for instance, I would expect less than a ten percent response rate, and not all those responses would be cordial.

I have found the overwhelming response on the Isle of Wight to be positive, and the frequency of a smile extraordinarily high. This is particularly and unexpectedly so for adolescent and teenage girls and even youths. To be greeted with a dazzling smile rather than a sulky glare can make my walk so much more pleasant, even if the well-wishers are only admiring the fortitude of an unimaginably old man who can still totter along the track.

~

I'm taking advantage of a bench erected in memory of a long-dead lady of local note. It sits under a mantle of oak boughs close to the river bank, and from it I like to watch the changes in form and shape of the river as the tide ebbs and flows.

At low tide the mudflats appear and attract a host of hungry diners. Sandpipers, Egrets and other long-legged birds wade ponderously in search of tit-bits; at high tide all sorts of species share the river, and mostly amicably.

It's just short of the turning of the tide and I admire the skill and power of a young man in a skiff. He is pulling apparently effortlessly at the oars and moving faster than I could run. Then a gentle puttering announces the approach of a water taxi from the marina at Yarmouth, The are no passengers to wave at, but the man standing at the tiller lifts an arm to acknowledge my greeting. He is wearing oilskins and a high-visibility life jacket. This is in stark contrast to a large middle-aged woman on a paddleboard. She looks as if she is hurrying to be back at her landing point by the bridge before the tide recedes and leaves her stranded. Despite the chilly conditions, she wears a summery floral dress. Her only concession to her situation is that she is wearing beach shoes and has left her designer heels in the car. I know this as I see her often, and she told me once that she enjoys being the centre of attention and people thinking she is potty.

~

In my time I have taken the Balkan mountain range in my stride and followed in the foot and hoof steps of Robert Louis Stevenson and his donkey Modestine through the glorious Cevennes of South-western France.

Today was the first time I found myself completely lost and panicking within a few hundred yards of civilisation. Night was falling, but I was loath to leave and had decided to take a walk on the wild side.

Mangrove trees are known as the 'roots of the sea' and are the only tree which can survive in salt water. Though not common, they can be found in some coastal wetlands in Britain. On the inland side of the track following the course of the Yar is a wide ditch filled with stagnant water, rotting wood and leaf mulch and the odd beer can. It is not seawater, but the rainwater which runs down from the raised fields and forms an odiferous morass from which poke interestingly deformed trees. They are certainly not mangroves, but when in the mood for fantasy I like to pretend they are, and that beyond the noxious swamps and thicket there lies a strange, exotic, sub-tropical land rather than a few hundred acres of Isle of Wight farmland.

Apart from the smell of the ditch and denseness of the thicket, lines of rusting barbed wires dissuades explorers, but earlier I saw a break in the fence and signs of a winding path leading through the thicket.

I took it and followed the path, the ooze reaching the tops of my hiking boots and disguising a network of intertwined roots. My plan was to spend ten minutes in previously untrodden territory, but I had not got far before the sky suddenly darkened and a great cawing and rustling and flapping of wings clutched at my heart. I steadied myself against a tree bough and saw that the light had been stolen by a mob of crows. I shouted an apology for disturbing them and tried to do it in Crowese, but they made no further response.

I like corvids in all their variety and particularly crows. Four arrive in the back garden each day to see what's on offer and have a wash and brush-up. One sits on the ridge of the roof to keep watch, while the others take turns to dunk themselves into the oversized bird bath. They are surprisingly dainty about their ablutions, and fly jauntily off as if refreshed when the watchbird has had its turn.

Like swans, they mate for life and stay faithful to their partners. They are amongst the cleverest of all avian species, adaptable and fearless. They can even mimic human speech, and I have watched videos on You Tube of a young woman allegedly having conversations with them.

Crows and rooks are hard to tell apart for amateurs

like me, but it is said that crows are usually seen alone while rooks like company. If that is so, it means the army of birds I sent up were rooks, which would explain why they did not reply to my greeting in Crow.

~

Ten minutes later and I was trudging up a sloping field. The going was getting harder and I was beginning to feel uneasy.

After a few hundred sludgy steps across a muddy field and away from the mangrove swamp, I decided there was not going to be much to see. Turning back, I thought I was retracing my steps until I arrived at a line of trees and a water-filled ditch that I had not encountered on the way out. It was either a time-slip or I had temporarily lost my way. The side of the ditch looked too steep and slippery to navigate, so I decide to jump across it. My walking pole was not long enough to vault across the gap, so I threw it over, backed up and then threw myself into space. I have vaulted across ditches aplenty in a long life, but had forgotten how many years ago I had taken on the previous one.

I almost made it, but stumbled and stepped back and slid down the slope into the water. Giving myself the look Oliver Hardy would give Stan Laurel, clambered out of the ditch and made my way back towards the river.

My next problem was that the Yar was not where I thought I had left it.

I had by now walked at least twice as far as I had travelled from the river, but stretching ahead of me in the gloom were only tree-lined fields. The only sign of human habitation were the lights of a huddle of cottages where I thought Freshwater should be. I sat down and considered my situation. Either my time-slip theory was true and I had returned to a previous age, or, more probably, I had lost my bearings. Then I realised what had happened. I had assumed that because the track, mangrove swamp and thicket followed the course of the river, so would the fields. This was not so, and I had wandered off course. I was tired, wet, cold and lost.

I pulled my phone out and thought about the humiliation factor of calling my wife and asking her to ask the emergency services to find and rescue me.

Pulling myself together and turning the phone torch on, I tossed a mental coin, turned right and set off in search of civilisation.

~

An hour later and I had walked at least a mile and crossed two more ditches and was still lost. Clearly, the majority of muddy and fallow fields look much the same, especially after dark. My new problem was that I had no way of communicating with the rest of the world. When the torch beam dimmed and went out, I had not realised this was because the battery was flat.

Beginning to panic, I decided I would have to try and find shelter for the night, or at least until my battery hopefully regained enough strength to text my wife. I gave myself another Oliver Hardy look, then followed a footpath to where a hedge barred my way, took off my knapsack, laid it on the ground and joined it.

~

'Hellaugh. Are you alright?'

The cultured tones came from where a circle of light had appeared alongside the hedge. A long-legged Jack Russell terrier was looking down its nose at me, as if deciding whether to bite or lick me.

The dog's owner turned the torch beam upon herself and I saw a middle-aged lady in a headscarf, Barbour jacket, twill trousers and green Wellington boots.

Thinking quickly, I said my phone battery had deadened and I was just changing it for my spare. Had she, I wondered, come from the riverside walk, and if so, could I join her to take advantage of her torch?

With a slightly bemused look, she said yes and yes, and I followed her alongside the hedge to a stile and kissing gate which shortly deposited us all of a hundred yards from where I had entered the mangrove swamp.

As we parted company, I made a mental note to never leave home without a compass, map and proper torch, even if going to the paper shop in the village in broad daylight.

∞∞∞∞

Making up the numbers

Times change, even on the Isle of Wight. According to the Census of 2011, there were 138,265 people living on the Island as compared with 80,000 a hundred years before. The average Islander's age in 2011 was 44, and 92.2 percent of residents were born in England. There were no figures for speakers of Wightean, but English was the chosen tongue of more than 98 percent. Other languages included Polish (0.3 percent) and Tagalog/Filipino at 0.2 percent. 761 chefs were living and working on the Island, compared with a mere 299 boat builders and repairers. Only fourteen leatherworkers and cobblers plied their trade here, although 9,508 Islanders walked daily to work. More than 280 arable and livestock farmers worked the land, which may explain why, after English, Polish was the most common language.

Most bizarre of all was the claim that there were 196 different 'ethnicities' living in harmony on the Isle of Wight. As the UK Government rules that there are just eighteen different ethnic groups, one assumes the towns, forests and backwaters of the Isle of Wight must have been awash with self-identifying Klingons, Druids and Vegan Vampires. When asked, 766 people said they identified as Jedi Knights and 17 claimed their religion was Heavy Metal.

Pyramid Selling

In strong competition for the Most Unlikely Book Title of the Year must be Egypt and the Isle of Wight. According to the author, the Island was colonised by Ancient Egyptians. As proof he offers the facts that 'yar' is Egyptian for 'river' and Medina a sacred Arabic city.

9

"The Two Great Cowes that in loud thunder roar
This on the eastern, that the western shore."

Charles Godfrey Leland, 19th-century American
humourist, folklorist and rubbish poet.

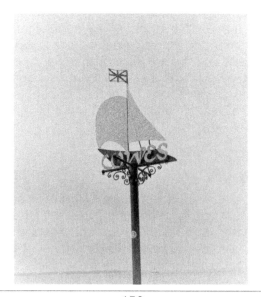

Many people misbelieve that summer begins with the longest day on June 21st

In fact, summer is on the wane by then, and officially starts on the first day of that month. Don't ask me why, but that's how it is.

Whatever the reason, today is also by long-standing tradition the day I give my shorts and legs their first airing of the year.

Shortly after the ceremony and a walk along the track, I suspect a few onlookers with sensitive natures, wished I had not made the change. The custom is that I wear my ultra - baggy (to ensure good ventilation) shorts every day till my knees get too cold to operate properly. Or my wife cannot bear the sight of what she says have begun to resemble two lumpy stacks of blue-veined Stilton cheese.

There was, though, another reason to mark and celebrate the date, as this morning we officially took possession of our allotment.

I'm now taking my ease in the shed, which is just as it should be, with an ill-fitting door, leaky roof and cracked window giving panoramic views of the distant downs. There's a frail kitchen chair and a lady's boudoir dressing table supporting a gas ring, old-fashioned kettle and supply of tea bags and dried milk. Coffee is not allowed on the premises as the only proper drink to have in an allotment shed is strong, cheap Indian tea in a stained, cracked mug.

On the shelf above is a selection of paperbacks that I have long meant to read but not got round to. They are too dog-eared and distressed to be given to a charity shop, so will eventually find use in the incinerator I have made by drilling holes in an old zinc-coated dustbin. It was only when I had made the holes that I realised the 'vintage' bin would probably have fetched enough at the new collectibles shop to pay for a state-of-the art purpose-built incinerator.

Although deeply seductive, my man-cave/shed is probably too comfortable and unsuitable a place in which to write. Roald Dhal and other illustrious authors did their best work in garden sheds, but I think I would find the view and surroundings too distracting.

Q: What's brown and comes steaming out of cows?
A: The Isle of Wight ferry

Very old and poor joke which only worked when spoken and when the ferries were brown.

Cowes is very much a town of two halves, in a physical as well as cultural sense.

The Medina river is not much more than a hundred yards across at the point where it empties into the Solent, but the spiritual distance between the halves of the town could not be wider. Like Prince or Picasso, the western half side is so confident in its superiority and celebrity that it doesn't bother with more than a one-word name.

Cowes is the home of the Royal Yacht Squadron, a host of trendy eateries and coffee and we-saw-you-coming souvenir and designer clothes shops. Any pound stores are either hidden from view or disguised as worthy charity shops.

Across the river like a poorer and ill-favoured

member of the same family lies East Cowes. It is an irony that while Cowes proper is alive with reminders of a seafaring heritage in the names of the saltier outlets, the other side of the river is where the real work on boats is done. Also ironically, the most upmarket holiday home in the world is sited in East Cowes, but more of that later.

Cowes was already a popular resort for the gentry when the Prince Regent's enthusiasm for sailing led to the first official regatta in 1812. Slotted in between the major horse racing events at Glorious Goodwood and the start of the annual grouse massacre on the 'Glorious' 12th of October, it quickly became a place to be seen whether or not you knew the difference between the sharp and blunt ends of a boat.

In more recent times, the late, great Prince Phillip was a regular competitor, and past Imperial visitors include the ill-fated Czar of all the Russias and his family. There's even a plaque on the prom marking the site of the first meeting in 1873 of American heiress Jenny Jerome and Lord Rudolph Churchill, whose offspring was the great wartime leader Winston. The eclectic roll-call of modern celebs who have been spotted at Cowes week include royally-connected Pippa Middleton, fashion model and pub-owner Jodie Kidd, former popster Simon Le Bon, actor Jeremy Irons and TV gardener, novelist and past winner of the prestigious Bad Sex Scene Award in Fiction, Alan Titchmarsh.

Something Cowes does have in abundance is fine buildings and lots of visitors, which is curious when you think about how little there seems to be to do there.

At last count there were two hundred self-catering venues on Airbnb. Even the most excellent local-knowledge Isle of Wight Guru site finds it hard to drum up much enthusiasm for the stony beaches, and its top ten things for visitors to do include a visit to the M&S food hall and a walk along the prom before a look at a museum of Classic Boats.

Probably because of the calibre and wealth of the Victorian *beau monde*, there is a complete variety of majestic Victorian homes overlooking the sea, ranging from massive villas to mock-Tudor fantasies. Towards the unfashionable end of the prom there's a growing phalanx of bland, cubist apartment blocks which would still set you back at least one arm and a leg and maybe two of each.

Hordes of monarchs and world-famous figures have visited Cowes, but my eye was caught by a blue plaque marking the birthplace of what I had for some reason previously thought to be a fictional figure.

On the quay and close to one of the finest art-deco apartment blocks I have seen is the one-time home of Thomas Arnold, son of a Cowes Customs Officer and headmaster at Rugby during the time of the *Tom Brown's Schooldays*.

Leading from the quay, a cutely winding and partly-cobbled precinct offers upmarket salty souvenirs and nautical attire, and a shop where you can buy all manner of 'artisan' products as well as 'hand-crafted' fair-trade baskets and cushions. Unsurprisingly, the charity shop displays garments which started life in very exclusive and pricey establishments.

One anomaly is a bench outside a shop which bears a notice saying it is only for the use of RNLI members. Needless to say, and though I was not at all in need of a rest, I plonked myself on it and waited to be confronted by the Official Monitor of the RNLI Bench. If there is one, he or she did not appear, and robbed me of the chance to deliver my carefully prepared riposte that I had raised enough money from RNLI drives at Portsmouth's radio station to buy and equip a lifeboat and its crew.

Apart from that peculiar exception, I find Cowes a welcoming, easy-on-the-eye and inoffensive sort of place. It does no harm, appeals to the latent snobbery in most of us, and is very popular with visitors who think they would just love to live there but probably would not.

Where I think I would quite like to live is the little stretch of coastline fronting the village of Gurnard. The remains of a delightful jumble of seen-better-days craft and old Mr Peggoty-style dwellings are still to be seen, but things are changing.

The inevitable and dread hand of progress is manifested in the apartment blocks and holiday homes vying for space, but at least the builders have made the effort to clad them in wood and paint them blue to try and fit in with the real thing.

Across the river and a very, very short voyage on the chain ferry (if it's working) Cowes's other half is a very different kettle of fish.

East Cowes has the feel and even smell of a no-nonsense, busy place that makes or made things to do with the sea. Not so long ago, some of those things were boats that operated on sea or in the air. Saunders-Roe was once the creator of flying boats, rockets and developed the first hovercraft.

Nowadays the company makes a great proportion of the giant wind turbine blades for other parts of the Kingdom, but none for local use as they are wisely not permitted on the Island.

Cowes may have been the birthplace of the future headmaster of Rugby and been graced by visits from czars, kings and pop stars, but East Cowes was the choice of home and workplace for many household names.

Architect John Nash built a home in East Cowes in 1798, hovercraft inventor Sir Christopher Cockerill lived and worked at East Cowes, as did inventor of the Dam Busters Bouncing Bomb', Barnes Wallis, while legendary boat builder and designer Uffa Fox was born and raised on that side of the river.

Perhaps a reason that some of the grimier parts of this side of the Medina remind me of Portsmouth is because of how East Cowes suffered in the bombing raids of World War II.

Across the water, three thousand lost their lives in Portsmouth as a result of the repeated raids on the home of the country's premier Naval Port. Almost a hundred people died in bombing raids on the Island, and seventy in East Cowes on the 4th of May, 1942.

The raid would have been even more deadly had there not been a Polish destroyer in port for a refit. In a breach of regulations, the captain had kept a supply of munitions on board, and used smoke canisters to obscure the Luftwaffe's intended target. He also employed the large-calibre guns of the Blyskawica to good effect, forcing the bombers to fly higher, thus losing accuracy. The loss of life and bravery and resourcefulness of the captain and his ship are remembered and commemorated every year.

~

A more than well-known royal couple chose to buy a holiday home in East Cowes, and were said to have preferred living there to their grand palace in London.

Queen Victoria and Prince Albert bought the Osborne estate in 1845 for the then princely sum of £28,000. The original house was too small for their purposes, so Albert by-passed the usual channels and, with professional help, designed and built a new one.

As holiday homes go it was quite substantial, with dozens of rooms and a full-sized cottage from Switzerland and a miniature fort in the grounds for the children to play with. The house stood in around two thousand acres of parklands, but being more used to royal dwellings the size of Buckingham Palace, Victoria referred to it as '…dear, modest, unpretentious Osborne.'

The couple shared their happiest times there, and when her beloved husband died at only 42 at Windsor Castle in 1861, Victoria fled to the Island even before his funeral took place. It was said that she slept with his nightshirt in her arms every night until her own death.

Victoria died at Osborne House on January 22, 1901 after sixty-three years on the throne. She had reigned so long that nobody alive knew the precise protocol following the death of a monarch, and chaos and confusion was said to have followed.

It was known that the Old Queen wanted a full military state funeral, with no embalming or laying-in-state. Moreover, she did not want mourning black, but a white funeral with white horses. Her coffin was made by a local shipwright and escorted across the Solent flanked by eleven miles of warships, firing salutes as the relatively tiny Royal yacht *Alberta* passed by.

Osborne House was gifted to the nation by King Edward VII and is open to the public.

I enjoy a visit to this reminder of our Imperial past, but the Victorian way of overstuffing of rooms and corridors and every available nook makes it seem less like a home and more like a museum.

To be fair I suppose that's what Osborne House is.

'I could live here...'

The Internet is awash with videos of clever and audacious squirrels busily raiding bird feeders and performing impressive acrobatic feats to overcome obstacle course and win a food prize.

They are, with rare exceptions, squirrels of the grey variety. Despite the ten acres of woodland over the fence, a sighting of a native red squirrel is a rare event, and we've still not managed to tempt one into the garden. The glass-fronted flip-top feeding box I filled with a special mix of tasty treats has been ignored, so either the local reds are very fussy eaters or very short-sighted. But, as I should have expected, the new and expensive feeder has not been neglected by the Badger Boys mob.

Since I put the box at the top of a six-foot pole it has been under siege. We watched through night-vision glasses as the pack leader- a huge creature we know as Big Boris - stood on his hind legs and shook the pole furiously till it broke and deposited the feeding box on to the ground. He then did a smash-and-grab raid through the glass panel and polished off the contents.

It's a fact that badgers have poor eyesight but acute hearing and sense of smell, and that they value peanuts even above a tasty earthworm. This means that Boris either smelled the mix in the elevated box or had inside information after hearing me telling my wife I had put the contents of a family-sized bag of roasted peanuts in with the mix to provide additional incentive to any alleged squirrels in the area.

When the coast is clear, I will treat the area around the feeder with some of my home-made badger repellent, but don't hold out much hope that it will deter Big Boris and his mates. If anything, it seems the overnight raids have increased since I started marking our borders with my pee. My wife now believes that, rather than putting them off, the acrid stink is actually attracting them.

~

Friday morning, and the big event is the weekly indoor market. Disappointed visitors from off the Island and unaware of how things are done here could probably sue the organisers under the Trades Description Act, but we like it for its predictability and lack of goods on offer.

The so-called market is staged in the village hall, and is always attended by the same villagers. The stalls are presided over by the same people, and some of the stuff on sale has been putting in an appearance since we arrived on the Island.

The tables bearing home-grown eggs and home-made cakes and biscuits and jams are always busy, but the others mostly offer the usual bric-a-brac that people look at but rarely buy. The routine has its own particular protocol as people who have known each other for years adopt the roles of sellers and (possible) buyers. Potential customers walk slowly round the tables, nodding and smiling and having a chat with the vendors as if they had not met in the Co-op earlier that morning. Some will pick up a rusty nutmeg grater or cassette of the *Best of Mario Lanza* before moving on. Another exception to the general rule is that the vendors never try and sell their products, and sometimes look irritated or concerned if you ask for a price. I suspect the owners don't really want to shift any of their products as they are here for the company and tradition, and not selling anything saves them the trouble of re-stocking. For whatever reason, I have seen the same displays on most of the bric-a-brac tables every week since my first visit. One has a dog-eared Bulgarian phrase book prominently displayed at a price more than it would cost in WHSmith. Every week I make an offer for it, and the little old lady seated behind her wares looks as shocked as if I had just farted before shaking her head and carrying on with her knitting.

Ironically, the busiest stand is one which seems to have a very modest turnover. On duty behind the rows of vegetable plants, herbs and sometimes exotic flowers will be a man with a long beard and an encyclopaedic knowledge of all forms of fauna and how best to grow and maintain them. His name is Robin, but we call him the Plant Doctor. Like any practitioner, he is always in demand. Every week there's a queue of non-customers asking for advice on a problem with their wilting wisteria or undersized onions. The problem is that while he is dishing out solutions, he is not taking money. If there was a case for putting a service on the rates, it would be the Robin's weekly surgery.

~

It is the evening of the open meeting concerning the siting of the new primary school, and my wife is taking photographs of me in the back garden. This is not because she wants to record the rare event of me changing out of my summer shorts and putting on a clean shirt and combing my hair. She is, in fact, compiling a selection of photographs for what actors like to call casting cards.

As revealed in the local paper, a TV thriller is to be shot on the Island and an agency is inviting applications for participants in the crowd scenes.

Dozens of 'extras' or background artists as they are more politely known nowadays will be needed, and the agency is asking for photographs of people of all ages and looks. My wife ridiculed the idea of my applying until she saw that neither age nor looks was a barrier, and that the fee was nearly a hundred pounds each day of filming. As she said, a hundred pounds is a lot more than I earn from a day in my office pretending to be working on a new novel or travel book. As I pointed out, doing extra work would be a bit of a come-down from my days as a radio DJ and voice-over specialist, but near-beggars cannot be choosers.

When I said how much fan mail I used to get from fans of my radio programmes, my wife reminded me that the majority had never seen me, and those who had often remarked how I had an excellent face for radio.

~

Bright and early on a Sunday morning, and I've been ferrying plants, tools, bunches of bamboo sticks, packets of seedlings and wheelbarrow loads of horse poo up to our new allotment. When I was a child in Portsmouth, a passing horse and cart would spark off a poo race, with synchronised door opening and a rush with bucket and shovel to be first to reap the rewards. Every house in our road had a small vegetable patch, and horse poo was highly valued. In our new location, we have a virtually inexhaustible supply, but I do get some odd looks from younger dog walkers who see me bent over a steaming heap of manure and must think I have a fetish about keeping the track outside our back gate poo-free.

~

A couple of hours later and I've made a start on surrounding the individual plots with planking to make raised beds. This is not to save us bending over an extra four inches, but so we can cover each plot with a thick layer of compost at the end of the growing season. In France we had several acres of friable, fertile soil to grow our food; here we will have to make the best use of every square metre and make sure we replace what we have taken from the earth. After much thought and the occasional harsh word, we have settled on rhubarb, beetroot, raspberries, strawberries and gooseberries, pumpkins, runner and broad beans, garlic and onion, leeks, swede and butternut squash. Not bad for a plot the size of our old sitting room in Brittany.

If we get it right, there will also be room for 'catch' crops like radishes. Potatoes and carrots will be grown in dustbins and old laundry bags against the fences, and the more delicate fruits and vegetables like melons and aubergines in the greenhouse.

There are three general rules governing what we choose to grow. One is to grow a lot of the things that would cost a lot more in the shops, which includes tomatoes and aubergines, strawberries and melons. The other is to pick fruit and vegetables which will like the type of soil. Then there's the yearly wild card ceremony, where we each choose something, we have not tried before.

I have heard allotment owners claim to get all their vegetable needs for the year for free, and even sell the surplus off for a profit. In our case and when allowing for seeds, bags of potting compost, fertiliser, new tools and the rent of our plot, we probably make a small loss on what the fruits of our labours would cost if we bought them in the local greengrocery.

At this point, many people (usually those who don't have an allotment) will tell you that food pulled from the earth and put on the table in the same day tastes so much better. Personally, I don't think that's true, not that it matters. The point of the exercise for us (as well as the benefits of the actual exercise) is to sow the seeds and see the first delicate shoots appear, then nurture them to maturity, watching over their progress like a doting parent. I don't know it is true that plants have feelings, but we both feel a pang of sorrow when one dies on us, and a small burst of joy when a weakly infant becomes a strong and healthy adult.

~

The sun is at its zenith and I am in the greenhouse, talking encouragingly to the tomato, squash and aubergine seedlings. I sit with dirt under my fingernails and a mug of tea to hand as the church bells ring out to remind the parishioners that they are still there and that in the midst of the pandemic there is hope for the future. Apart from the bells there is not a sound, then an impatient screech tells me Phil the pheasant is sitting on the shed roof waiting for his breakfast.

Although the alleged squirrel is still ignoring the feeding box, Phil has become another mouth to feed and knows where to find me when I am not in the back garden.

Probably introduced into Britain by the Romans, pheasants became briefly extinct in the 17th century. Nowadays, they are said to be amongst the most common bird species and more than forty million birds are carefully and expensively bred and then released each year to be slaughtered. Luckily for them, most of the people who spend hundreds of pounds a day for the pleasure of killing them are rotten shots, so millions escape into the wild. They live and roost in woodlands like ours, and one cock can have a dozen or more females in his harem. They proclaim ownership and territory with a harsh, two-syllable call. Once male pheasants have taken food from humans, they lose their shyness; Phil is anything but shy and will eat quite happily from my palm.

I hold up a hand in apology and reach for the birdseed box. Although I would rather be in France than Freshwater and not have a garage in danger of collapsing and a house sliding downhill to join it, I reflect on how good life can be in this quiet corner of the Diamond Isle.

~

A phone call distracts me as I am laying down my daily badger deterrent at one of their favourite entry points. I zip up, wipe off the toecaps of my gardening boots and answer it in the summerhouse.

My caller introduces herself as the head of the Island's premier agency for actors, walk-on artists and general entertainers. After her call, I think about calling back to see if it is a hoax, then go down to tell my wife that the casting agency for the TV thriller to be filmed on the Island want me to test for a proper acting part.

'So, what's the part?' my wife asks, 'a bloated corpse dragged out of the sea? A fairly lifelike scarecrow, or the village drunk?'

'I'll have you know,' I say, drawing myself up to my full height, 'it's for a local businessman, and it's a speaking part.'

'Hmmm,' she responds. 'What sort of business-man? A sort of cross between Del Boy and Arthur Daly? And how many lines do you have to remember?'

'He-Leo-is a successful businessman, my agent tells me,' I say, savouring the words 'my agent'. 'And it's what we in the business call a cameo role.'

'How many lines?' she repeated.

'Two', I say defensively, 'but they both have more than one sentence.'

'Okay,' my wife says with a smirk, 'I suppose you might be able to remember two lines with enough practice. And if you can't, I suppose you could have them written down on a piece of paper off-camera. What do they call them? 'She looks puzzled for a moment, then says: 'Ah yes, it's what you call "idiot boards" in the business, is it not?'

∞∞∞∞

Celebrity Island

Despite modern-day reservations about the Isle of Wight as a cultural hotbed or celebrity magnet, the long list of noteworthy people who lived, worked or spent time in the Isle of Wight includes:

Queen Victoria, who bought a holiday home on the Island in 1845

Charles Dickens, who stayed and wrote at Bonchurch in 1849

Winston Churchill who visited his sister at Ventnor in 1888

King Charles I, who was a captive for a year in Carisbrooke Castle

Charles Darwin began Origin of the Species at the King's Head hotel

Isaac Pittman wrote his shorthand dictionary while staying on the Island

Lewis Carroll gathered material for Alice in Wonderland here

Oscar Wilde arrived in 1884 to lecture on fashion and have a photograph taken

Architect *John Nash* built a home in East Cowes in 1798

Revered Victorian poet *Algernon Swinburne* lived and is buried at Bonchurch

Poet Laureate *Alfred Lord Tennyson* lived for many years at Freshwater

Communist philosopher *Karl Marx* visited the island on several occasions

Guglielmo Marconi conducted his earliest experiments near the Needles

Earl Mountbatten of Burma was the last Governor of the Island

American poet *Henry Wadsworth Longfellow* visited Shanklin in 1868

Inventor of the 'Bouncing Bomb' *Barnes Wallis* worked at East Cowes

Poet *Alfred Noyes* lived at Undercliff and died there in 1959

John Keats visited the island twice, firstly in 1817

Author *J B Priestley* lived at Brook for many years

Handbag designer and sexy sigher *Jane Birkin* grew up at Brook

Hovercraft inventor *Sir Christopher Cockerill* lived and worked at East Cowes

Rugby headmaster *Thomas Arnold* was born at Cowes

Novelist *Philip Norman* attended Ryde School and wrote books about the Island

Film actor and raconteur *David Niven* spent part of his childhood at Bembridge

Diary impresario *Thomas Letts* moved to the Island in 1859 and lived in Chale

Margaret Thatcher rented a home on the Island at the coastal village of Seaview

After leaving The Shadows, bass guitarist *Jet Harris* lived in a cottage at Bembridge

Jack Douglas of 'Carry On' film fame married a local girl and lived and died in Newport

Dad's Army star *Bill Pertwee* and TV's *Shaw Taylor* were neighbours in Totland

Newsreader *Kenneth Kendal* lived in Cowes

∞∞∞∞

10

*"Every little valley lies
Under many-clouded skies;
Every little cottage stands
Girt about with boundless lands;
Every little glimmering pond
Claims the mighty shores beyond"*

Victorian poet, author of *The Highwayman*
and Island resident Alfred Noyes

The fields, hedgerows and woodlands threatened to explode with life.

Winged visitors wheel and soar above as if in celebration, and wildflowers garland the track up Golden Hill.

In the back garden, the fruits of summer are a-blush and a-glow. Despite being wrenched from their home soil and ferried across the Channel, our plum trees are showing signs of emerging from stasis. Gooseberry, black current, blueberry and cherry bushes and trees promise much, and Yan and Gwynana the Breton goldfish have surfaced to see what all the fuss is about.

Across the track, the allotmenteers have emerged from their hibernation, and horse shit will be in short supply ere long.

Then as I contemplate the contented scene, something changes, and I realise the songbirds have stopped singing. A shadow passes across the surface of the pond and I squint up towards the sun. Slowly and majestically wheeling high above is a buzzard, and probably our local buzzard. He appears over the allotment every day, but this is the first time I have seen him directly above the garden.

We value a bird sighting by its rarity, and pigeons and kingfishers are at opposite ends of the points scale. Buzzards are the commonest of our birds of prey, but it is still a thrill to see one sitting majestically on a telegraph pole or soaring lazily overhead. The common buzzard has a wingspan of more than a metre and feeds on small mammals and birds, and their call is a high-pitched shriek or sometimes like the mewling of a discontented cat.

I see there is a pattern to its cruising, and having completed a circle directly overhead it moves on to our neighbours garden. The routine continues until the great bird disappears in the direction of Tennyson Downs, and the sparrows, tits, finches and buntings find their voices and take back possession of their garden. I don't know if they see or sense danger from above, but clearly they know when death is on the wing.

~

Our neighbours stand outside their front doors, heads bowed. It's re-cycling day, and the green bins along the pavement somehow look as if they too are lined up to pay their respects to Jack. The cul-de-sac is narrow, and the dustcart often has a problem squeezing between parked cars. I glance at my watch and see it's about the time that the big green vehicle lumbers round the corner into the Close, and I can't help thinking about what will happen if there's a confrontation and Jack will be late for his own funeral.

Our neighbours' door opens and Mary comes out, leaning on the arm of a tall young man who I assume is one of her grandsons. They walk slowly down to the where the hearse is parked and Mary stands looking through the window at the simple light-coloured coffin. She reaches out and puts a hand on the side window, then is helped back to a waiting car. The hearse moves off, a short man in an oversized tail coat leading the way. He has a top hat balanced in the crook of one arm, and walks with a measured tread. It is a solemn moment. Then I hear a muted roar in the distance, and see that the dustcart has arrived. Thinking quickly, the driver pulls into a side road and switches the engine off. The men in their orange overalls line up alongside the cart and doff their beanies and ball caps.

As we walk to our newly-washed car, I wonder what Mary is thinking as she follows her husband on his last journey, and how it will be for either Donella or myself when the time comes. For Mary it is the end of more than sixty years of togetherness and she will be alone until it is time to re-join him. Of course it is the natural cycle of life and death and comes to us all, but I cannot think that makes it any easier for those left behind.

~

It's inarguable that the French are generally brilliant at outdoor food markets, but rubbish at boot sales.

Apart from the big, organised town *brocantes* (mostly old furniture) and *marchés aux puces* (literally 'flea markets') they genuinely don't seem to get the concept of setting up shop outdoors to flog their unwanted household items.

In contrast and though they are catching up, outdoor British food markets can be quite limp affairs, while our boot sales can be spectacular occasions and offer everything from a pair of shoes to a car or coffin.

Sadly, our weekly boot sale is as limited and dull an affair as the Friday indoor market. Even in the best weather there will be no more than a handful or two of cars lined up on the common. When it's wet, cold or miserable, nobody bothers. Most of the things on sale will be the usual selection of items that the owners have tired of or replaced because they are broken. Some will offer plants and seedlings or bunches of rhubarb, and my favourite is the Men in Sheds table. It will be groaning under the weight of second or third hand hammers and saws and even the odd wooden plane or spokeshave tools. I already have at least two of everything I will ever need, but, like some women with shoes and handbags, I believe a man can never have too many tools.

Today was sunny and dry and a couple of dozen tables had been set up, only just outnumbering the visitors. The vendors have the same selling (or non-selling) technique as at the indoor market, and are often the same people. On the mainland it's sometimes hard to get past a stall without being accosted. Here, the vendors make no more effort than to give a grave nod or even avoid eye contact.

An exception is a man with a large white van and a loud voice. The first time we met, he said his wife had just died so he was selling their possessions to help pay for her funeral. He was in the same spot for the next four weeks, so it must have been a very expensive funeral.

~

It looks like the fight to claim the location of West Wight's new primary school is getting serious.

When we arrived at the boot sale, a posse of young mums had gathered at the entrance, wearing sloganised tee-shirts and collecting signatures for a petition to keep the children and school at Freshwater. There was talk of angry letters to the local papers, street protests and even marches upon the Newport council chambers. Then came the threat of physical confrontation when a couple of smartly-dressed young women arrived in a gleaming Range Rover. When they got out, their tee-shirts showed they were supporting Yarmouth for the new school location. They had deliberately entered enemy territory and had had the audacity to come equipped with clipboards to gather names for their petition. Led by a tall and very large young mum with whom I would not want to tangle, the local posse moved in and I thought there would be trouble. Luckily and after some sharp exchanges and a glance at the large lady's meaty and tattooed forearms, the Yarmouth contingent made a tactical withdrawal.

I'm sporting an unusual combination of clothing, even for me. Above the waist I look like a well-heeled spectator at Henley Regatta; below it I look as if I would be refused membership of a rough-sleeping community on the grounds of unacceptable scruffiness.

My hair has been trimmed and subdued by my wife, though I turned down her offer of a dye guaranteed to turn the greyest of hair into a shade of auburn. I did, however, accept her offer of a mascara brush and some neutral face makeup to tone down the glaring redness of my nose and cheeks from over-exposure to the sun and, perhaps as she alleges, the odd glass of Merlot.

My upper half is encased in a striped blazer I wore for a TV advert and was given by the production company because they said it was too big and gaudy to be any good for future use, especially after I had spilled most of my celebratory post-shooting Mutton Vindaloo down the front.

At my throat is a spotty red cravat, tucked into a gleaming white shirt, while my bottom half is clad in my favourite pair of gardening shorts and cut-off welly boots.

The reason for the dressing-up is my screen test for a speaking part in the TV thriller which starts production on the Island next month.

I filmed myself head-and-shoulders on the track with my phone on the end of a selfie stick, so had no need to worry about what I wore on my bottom half. This was not strictly true, as I startled a passing line of riders and their mounts when I emerged from the back gate. They were led by the lady who saw me peeing on a badger entry point last month, but I think she is used to my eccentricities. Perhaps she thought my appearance was evidence of a split personality, or I was filming a clip to send off to a website which caters for people with unusual dress tastes.

~

The screen test has been uploaded and sent to my agent. The part for which I am auditioning is Leo, 'a businessman'. I was given no direction as to what sort of business he was in, or his character or accent, so played him as an over-the-top type with a loud voice and expressive face. My wife said all I had to do was be myself and read the words, but it is not as easy at that. Though I have voiced hundreds of radio advertisements and appeared in a number of TV commercials and productions, this would be the first time I would have to act and speak at the same time without being able to read from a script. I did try to memorise the two lines by speaking them aloud before the filming session, but caused a stir when I asked the elderly lady in Edward G Robinson's paper shop for a large gin and tonic and complimented her on her cute bottom.

~

According to the local tourist board, the Isle of Wight is one of the sunniest places in the United Kingdom, with an average 37 hours a week. This compares with the national average of a paltry 29 hours. Ventnor is said to be the sunshine capital of the Island, and is claimed to exceed the weekly tally for Spain. This may or may not be true and I suspect the Spanish Tourist Board and the half a million Britons who have made a life there would beg to differ.

A bracing day at Steephill Cove, Ventnor

Apart from elevated sea views and ready access to good food and pubs (and allegedly the odd recreational drug) an added attraction for ramblers, riders, dog walkers and general landscape lovers is that the town sits below the St Boniface Downs.

One of many Island locations I find more than reminiscent of the west country, this voluptuous swathe of elevated moor and grasslands is accessed by a winding and narrow lane bestrewn with cattle grids to let you know you are in proper, working countryside rather than just a tarted-up beauty spot.

The Island was one of the last places in England to be converted to Christianity, and the Downs are named for the saint formerly known as Winfrith. Local legend has it that Winfrith preached in nearby Bonchurch from the aptly-named Pulpit Rock in 710. The change of name came about when Winfrith visited the Pope and was given the Boniface moniker and the Holy Father's blessing to go on a 35-year missionary trail. He was very good at it, and along with a huge tally of conversions, Boniface is also credited with replacing the pagan Oak of Thor with the pine as the symbol of a Christian Christmas.

Martyrdom came at the ripe old age of 80 when he was murdered by a band of brigands in the Netherlands, and a grand cathedral encloses his tomb in Fulda in central Germany.

The Bonchurch Festival was built around his Saint's Day, when the rediscovered wishing well named for him and located on the Downs is garlanded with flowers.

At 241 metres the garlanded St Boniface Downs are the highest on the Island and, the panoramic views are truly stunning. From here you can see from Beachy Head to the east, the Isle of Portland to the west and northwards to Portsmouth. As well as drinking in the views, you can also walk for almost ever on the skein of footpaths which seemingly connect the Downs with everywhere else on the Island. But tread carefully as here is the home of the largest cricket to be found in the entire kingdom

~

For all or most of the above reasons and some of which I am not quite sure, I like Ventnor almost enough to want to live there*.

When we started looking for a new home on the Island, I thought that - if we had to move from France - it would be a good place to move to. I liked the sense of history and fine and sometimes quirky architecture, the long walks above and below the town, the bustle and the ratio of pubs to people. You get the feeling that Ventnorians know how to enjoy themselves. Despite myself, I also like the feeling of 'edginess', which is how trendy people like to describe a place with a higher-than-average proportion of social dissonance and misbehaviour.

Then my wife pointed out that the reason we moved to France was to escape from living in places like Portsmouth and its smaller relations, of which Ventnor is a good example. Full of noise and traffic and too many young people who drive madly and take drugs and drink too much and probably sacrifice new-born children during regular Evil-worshipping gatherings in the Corporation gardens.

The reason I had a soft spot for Ventnor, she said, was it reminded me of my misspent youth.

As to origins, Ventnor started life as a fishing village in the 19th century and quickly became a very fashionable resort. Unlike many other towns which have lost their past, you can screw up your eyes and see the fine ladies with their waspy waists and posh bonnets and parasols being escorted by self-satisfied bourgeoisie husbands or skint gigolos as they showed off their finery on the promenade, Winter Gardens or manicured park.

Unlike west Wight and the Osborne house factor,

Ventnor became such a popular place with the *beau monde* because of its climate. So many wealthy Londoners bought holiday homes here that it became known as 'Mayfair-by-the Sea' and the 'English Mediterranean'.

Of course, lots of places in search of summer visitors, second-home owners and retirees like to bill themselves as having a micro-climate. It's usually an easily disproved gimmick dreamed up by PR departments, but in Ventnor's case it happens to be true. Allegedly. Although not at the most southerly point, the town's sheltered location beneath the lofty downs is the reason it can claim a record sunshine hours tally. The climate also allows the flourishing of sub-tropical plants, as evidenced at the former sanatorium which is now the Botanical Gardens.

I also like the variety Ventnor offers. On the downs you can walk for miles in harmony with nature and untroubled by roads. At the bottom of a corkscrew road is the predictably and understandably commercial promenade, though the amusement arcades are being steadily replaced by blocks of expensive apartments. One of my favourite hidden places on the Island is in Ventnor, and perhaps because it is only accessible by foot.

*Celebrated poet laureate and witty observer John Betjeman was not a big fan of Ventnor, and remarked how 'little Osbornes' were built on every available piece of cliff and that '...each little Osborne had its garden of palms, myrtles and hydrangeas and its glimpse of the sea.'

Tucked away beneath the Undercliff area, Steephill Cove is a mix of natural beauty and clever commercial exploitation. The sea still pounds away at the rocky shores as it has for a few million years, and there are no Costa Coffee signs, street lights or yellow lines. Instead, there are a number of quirkily delightful places where you can eat and drink and look out across the timeless waves. The old fishermen's cottages are still in place and live up to the quaintness of their names. Of course, things inside have changed a bit since the original occupants were in situ. The rental properties offer facilities and furnishings and fittings that even the most privileged of Victorian villa owners would have thought of as unimaginable luxury.

~

More news of the battle for the new primary school, and it's not good.

A week ago there was general rejoicing when it was announced that the council had decided that the new school would be built at Freshwater. Celebrations turned to howls of anger when the Yarmouth proponents said they would be taking legal action. This immediately caused the Council to put matters on hold while they reviewed the situation. And so, the threat of expensive law suits does make cowards of us all.

~

Not having heard from my agent about my screen test, I called her office.

She said the casting agency had not been in

touch, and sympathetically agreed that I have probably not got the part. She added that she hoped I did not put too much effort into learning my lines, and I said I will probably never forget them.

She laughed and said that is not unusual, especially when actors have not got the part they auditioned for. As if out of spite and to remind them of their failure, the word worms can sit in their brains forever. She promises to phone the casting agency and find out if they have made a decision and will let me know as soon as she does. If it is bad news, she is sure she can find me some background artist work.

I am sulking in my shed.

Although it was only a couple of sentences, the prospect of my first proper acting role had taken on a significance beyond its importance. It might, as I said to my wife, have been the start of a lucrative career or even sideline as an actor specialising in older roles. When Donella said it would, given my age and physical condition, probably be a short career, I pointed out that Clint Eastwood is 90 and going strong, and Mel Brooks, Gene Hackman and Dick Van Dyke are even older.

I suppose that a good part of my disappointment is because I have often thought I should have gone for acting rather than writing for a living. It's true that, as my wife says, there are as many unsuccessful actors as writers and I have been successful at what I chose to do. But as I replied with some degree of bitterness, when they do work, actors get paid. Authors can spend six months on a book which will bring them in less in royalties than a road-digger earns in a week. Not that I have anything against navvies, especially as I have been one, along with brewers' drayman, bouncer, publican, pickled onion manufacturer and the world's only professional bed-tester.

Also, apart from lighthouse-keeping and being a hermit, writing is the most solitary of professions. I have always been gregarious and enjoyed entertaining people, or as my wife likes to say, showing-off. Then, like most people, I arrived at a signpost which, had I taken the right direction, would have led to a very different life.

~

It is 1974, and I am approaching the grandiose entrance to Southsea's tired but still prestigious Queens Hotel.

As I reach the bottom of the steps, a wild-eyed character bursts through the doors and throws himself into my arms. He is babbling and drooling and begs me to save him from 'them' and make them let him stay. I carry him up the steps and deposit him at the top, then realise I have been cuddling Keith Moon, drummer for The Who rock band. He is so distressed, I learn, because the management objected to him letting off a thunderflash practice grenade in the toilet bowl of his luxury suite.

As I sympathise, he goes rigid, lets out a piercing shriek, stumbles down the steps and pursues a passing seagull in the direction of the seafront.

I watch him causing chaos on the road as he dashes across, then enter the hotel in time to see veteran comedian Ted Ray being carried up the ornate staircase by two burly hotel employees. I don't think the star of the popular radio show Ray's A Laugh is in the film in which I hope to make a fleeting appearance, but many of the movie's stars are staying at the Queens.

Based on a 'rock opera' by The Who, *Tommy* is about a blind, deaf and dumb boy who becomes a pinball champion and religious leader. The film featured a near-firmament of stars which, as well as The Who band members, includes Elton John, Tina Turner and Jack Nicholson.

Unless my walk-on part as a bouncer is consigned to the cutting room floor, I will have my moment of fame and be able to name-drop Elt, Tina and other acting colleagues for the rest of my life.

I am visiting the hotel because I have a date with another of the movie's stars, Swedish singer, dancer and actress Ann-Margret. She does not know we have a date, but on the set today I over heard her say she might be in the hotel bar this evening.

As it transpires, she is not in the Brandy Bubble cocktail lounge, but Roger Daltrey is. The Who's singer is behind the bar, holding a cocktail shaker and a bottle of something green. Watching him in impatient anticipation are his fellow band members minus Keith Moon, and a small, tubby, bearded man I think I should recognise.

Frowning, Roger Daltrey looks up as I enter and asks if I know how to make a Tequila Sunrise.

'Yep,' I say, 'but not like that.'

I am ordered to get mixing, then invited to join the party. Taking a seat beside him, I realise the diminutive bearded man is Ken Russell, the director of the film in which I hope to make an appearance. We sit and drink and talk, then I feel a presence and turn to see it is another star of the film. Oliver Reed is known to like a drink and a fight, and is swaying as he regards me with a distinct air of animosity. I get off the bar stool and turn to face him, and he lurches forward till our noses are almost touching. He continues to glare at me, then raises a large fist.

'I don't like the look of your face,' he slurs in his oddly unsuitable cultured voice, '-and I'm going to change it.'

I look at the pub brawl scar running from the corner of his mouth, then take a step back to give myself room.

As I prepare to defend myself, a large figure appears and drags Ollie back and out of range. It is Reg, his faithful minder, who apologises and announces that all my drinks this evening will be on Mr Reed.

~

Much later and I am propping up the Glasgow bar when Ken Russell asks if I have ever done any acting. When I say no, he says I should take it up as I have the looks and what he calls presence.

I look like a younger Oliver Reed, he says, and he is sure I would be much less trouble directing. If I like the idea, I should give him a call when filming is finished and he will find me something to get started.

As it happened, I was paid off for my extra work the next day and never went back to the set. After the long night with him at the bar and ending with a skinny dip from Southsea beach, I woke up to find I had lost Ken Russell's phone number. He was meanwhile busy wrapping up the movie and filming Southsea Pier burning down. So, instead of becoming a famous film star by usurping Ollie Reed, I went off to play at running radio stations.

More than fifty years have passed since then, and, after the lack of response to my audition tape, it looks like an actor's life is definitely not going to be for me.

∞∞∞∞

11

"Our window looks over house tops and cliffs on to the sea. So that when the ships sail past the cottage chimneys you may take them for weathercocks. We have Dale, forest and Mead and plenty of Lobsters."

English Romantic poet John Keats, writing in appreciation of the view from his cottage in Sandown in 1819.

Midsummer, but only the privileged, foolhardy or thoughtless will be enjoying a foreign break. At home, the Island is still in the lowest ranking of Covid 19 infections, and our restaurants, hairdressers and pubs are open and full.

This makes some Islanders wary rather than smug, especially of visitors from the mainland. A report in the local paper said that the level of drunken and violent behaviour has soared, and the cause is the invasion of so-called booze cruisers.

Once, the Channel ports of France were a popular destination for groups of young men in search of cheap drinks and a bit of fun. Now it seems they are crossing the Solent rather than the Channel to take advantage of the non-curfewed opening times. It is true that they bring not only money and mis-behaviour with them, but the threat of infection. There have been letters to the paper and petitions demanding that the ferries be closed and the Island become a fortress, but the protestors have forgotten that it is just not pleasure-seekers who use the ferries. The Island grows a lot of its own vegetables, but we would soon be on a more restricted diet than during the last War if the convoy of supply lorries did not make the daily crossing.

~

If there were a striking clock within earshot, it would be sounding midnight.

I am in the heart of the woodland beyond our fence, keeping company with my friend Ent, the fallen tree. There's a smuggler's moon and all is quiet except for the occasional grunt, snuffle and rustle from the creatures of the night.

I've been on my nightly rural Deliveroo-style supper run, and on the menu was a chicken carcass, some stale bread pudding and the furry remains of a pot of Ardennes pâté. As a special treat I included a handful of chocolate-covered peanuts I found down the back of the sofa and which were too far gone for even me to eat. They had lain there since last Christmas, but I don't suppose the badgers will mind them being past their best-by date.

With the longer days, suppertime comes ever later as I have to wait for the coast to be clear of dog walkers and their scavenging pets. But it is good to be here, and the later the hour the more content I feel to be at large and alone in this magical place.

I also like to think that the small hours are a good time to commune with the fallen tree. I know of course that the giant oak is dead, but it is, I like to kid myself, possible its spirit lives on. The Ancients believed that all trees had spirits, and oak trees were home to Dryads. When abroad at night they took the form of beautiful young women, and I live in hope of encountering one after dark so she could tell me of life in Ancient Greece.

Suddenly there is a movement in the thick undergrowth on the other side of the small clearing and then the sound of breaking branches as a figure emerges. I switch on and focus my torch and see that it is not a Dryad or woodland nymph, but Big Boris.

It is well-known that rabbits and foxes stay frozen to the spot when caught in a powerful torch beam; this is why 'lamping' is a favoured night-time activity for poachers or cullers. Boris does not move or react when the light falls on him, but I think this is not because he is frightened. It is because he chooses not to move.

We regard each other across the clearing for what seems a long time. I don't know how quick-witted or intelligent badgers are, and wonder if is considering thanking me for tonight's takeaway treat or teaching this intruder into his domain a lesson. Just in case it is the latter, I lift my free hand and give a nervous and hopefully placatory wave. I don't expect him to wave back, but hope he may recognise me by my smell and know me as a friendly source of food.

The tableau remains in place for no more than a minute, but seems longer. Finally, Big Boris turns his head to one side while still regarding me impassively. Then he lets out a low grunt, turns and disappears. If I didn't know better, I would say he gave an unconcerned shrug before making off, almost as if deciding I was no threat and he did not think it worth crossing the clearing to sort me out.

I let out a long sigh, switch off the torch and reach for my flask. It's my first really close encounter with a badger and my pulse rate has soared. They are not known for wanton savagery, but their rep was not helped by a grisly murder in Derbyshire a couple of years ago. Having murdered a pensioner, the killer dismembered the body and fed the pieces down the holes of a badger sett. The evidence disappeared in hours.

As I have found, badgers are shy creatures and more interested in earthworms and peanuts and Mars bars than human flesh. Even so, I'm glad Big Boris decided not to bite the hand that feeds him.

~

It must be like this in a particularly arid summer in Arizona.

After the wettest winter on record, a fickle Dame Nature has turned off the tap. The unusual mix of clay over sand in this area means footpaths and fields can become a sea of mud in the rainy season, yet rock-hard after even a short dry spell. Then come the fissures which make the cracks in our garage look like hairline fractures. The drying out of the ground is particularly noticeable in our back garden. This is because the thirsty roots of the trees over the fence soak up any water making its way down Golden Hill. As my friendly surveyor said, this is a good thing in the wet season, but not necessarily in a prolonged dry spell.

The house must be reacting to the change, as the Crack of Doom in my study has closed, the master bedroom door now opens and shuts quite normally, and the door to the shower room no longer swings eerily open if not properly closed. This, we have found, can be quite unnerving for guests sitting on the toilet.

~

I don't want to make a mountain out of a molehill, but it can't be a coincidence that the Latin name for a new squatter in our garden also forms the basis for *molestus* and *molesta*, as in 'annoying', tiresome' and 'troublesome'.

We are not big on billiard-table lawns and like to leave the grassy bits of our garden to nature. The occasional eruption from beneath is no problem, and earth that has been through a mole's excavating machinery makes fine potting soil. But our current visitor digs like he is on some form of chemical stimulant and likes to do things the hard way.

The other day I splashed out on some concrete

stepping stones and about a half a ton of shingle to make a dry and stable passageway around the summerhouse. The next morning, I found great mounds of soil had erupted through the gravel and the slabs all askew. It looked like a deliberate act of vandalism, as if the creature responsible was unhappy with me making his job harder. Hopefully it was my imagination, but it also looked as if the summerhouse itself was tilting slightly to one side. There's a four-inch raft of reinforced concrete holding it up, but I have seen what damage these cute little animals can do.

Moles have small cylindrical bodies with inconspicuous ears and eyes and reduced hind limbs and are famously short-sighted. To help them be good at what they do for a living they have powerful forelimbs and paws with an extra 'thumb' adapted for the most effective digging. Unlike badgers, moles don't eat plant bulbs, but their tunnelling activities cause damage to the soil. Mole 'runs' are actually not for getting around without being seen, but very effective worm traps. Sensing when an earthworm falls into the tunnel, the mole may choose to kill and eat it or use a toxin in its saliva to paralyse and store the victim for later enjoyment. Some mole larders have been found with a thousand worms awaiting their fate. These small but highly efficient predators are solitary creatures and avoid each other, but are naturally territorial and can become involved in fierce fights with rivals. Now it is me with a fight on my hands.

Calling in a mole catcher can be costly, and anyway I want to be the one to give the invader his marching orders. He is my mole so it is down to me to give him the elbow. Methods of getting rid of moles vary from unlikely country lore to modern technology.

Apart from paying up for an expert, the most reliable system seems to be to entice your mole into a humane trap. You then either kill it or, presumably, blindfold and release it to set up home in someone else's garden.

Amongst the traditional methods and one favoured by allotment holders everywhere is plastic bottles on sticks. It's believed that the vibration caused by the wind scares the mole away. Our allotment is awash with lines of upside-down milk and fizzy drink containers. Whether they work or the mole just hasn't got round to visiting them nobody can know. From my experiments, our mole is either deaf or is unconcerned by the noise. Another solution along the same lines is planting children's windmills where you don't want the intruder to venture, but a dozen ringing the summerhouse have had no effect. But there is another alleged way of persuading Mr Mole to move on, and it is a familiar one.

Perhaps to make up for their near-blindness, it seems that moles have an acute sense of smell. The proposal is that squirting human urine into their underground network will persuade them to seek sweeter-smelling pastures. As with badger repellent, it must be male pee and the older and smellier the better. The urine not the donor, that is.

If the wheeze works, it occurs to me that there could be an additional bonus and help with our cash-flow problems. Some companies charge ridiculous amounts for a bottle of ordinary water. I could market and flog Mole-B-Gone (plus secret ingredient X) with a money-back guarantee, and it might actually do the trick. As my wife says, my badger repellent smells bad enough in the open air. In a tunnel it would be sure to send the poor little creatures scrabbling for a breath of fresh air.

~

Although separate towns, Sandown and Shanklin are, like the two Cowes, close to but very different from each other.

Both are resorts and sit almost cheek-to-cheek three miles along the coast from Ventnor, though nowadays each has a distinctly different feel and appeal.

The Romanticism Movement and Romantic Era began in the second half of the 18th century, and the thirst for natural and scenic beauty helped transform Shanklin from a sleepy village to a popular destination for aesthetes to stand and wonder at the famous Chine.

According to the experts and excepting Dorset, the Isle of Wight is the only place where a narrow ravine with water running down it may be called a chine. It is alleged that some place on the Island lay claim to a chine when what they actually have is a cliff face collapse or even a broken water pipe. But Shanklin's is the real thing. Poet and leading light in the Romanticism John Keats was an admirer, and composed a catchy little ditty in its honour during his stay at Eglantine Cottage from 1817-19.

"The wondrous Chine is a very great lion, I wish I had as many guineas as there have been spyglasses in it."

Not particularly inspiring prose, perhaps, but the Chine has indeed attracted millions of visitors in the two centuries since he put pen to paper in praise of this natural phenomenon.

Another poet of renown and admirer of the town was American Henry Wadsworth Longfellow, who created the ultimate PR puff when the author of *The Song of Hiawatha* wrote in 1868 that Shanklin was 'one of the quaintest and loveliest places in the kingdom.'

Also a fan of Shanklin (if not Freshwater). Charles Darwin worked on *Origin of Species* here in 1858.

Development of the town as a quality resort continued apace with a promenade being built, bathing machines appearing on the sandy beach and fishermen renting out their boats for pleasure trips. The pier arrived in 1891, much to the displeasure of those who feared an invasion of 'trippers'. They were in fact accurate with their forecasts, and Shanklin became one of the most popular destinations on the Island.

Longfellow was certainly on the money when he described Shanklin as 'quaint', and the old part of the town with its thatched pubs and tea gardens is still a magnet for visitors with a camera to hand. Looking at the photographs of Old Shanklin, it seems a shame they could not have kept it exactly as it was, with horse and carts the only vehicles allowed on the cobbled streets. Impractical perhaps, but I bet it would be even more popular that way.

'New' Shanklin has one of the most extensive and popular shopping roads in that part of the Island, and generally has a bustling, friendly air. Unless, as we found, you venture into the wrong pub on the wrong evening and find yourself witnessing a witless scuffle. But that can happen anywhere...even on the Isle of Wight.

Once a prime location for hotels and eating places and arcades, the promenade at Shanklin is now lined with increasingly upmarket blocks of flats. It is an attractive, bustlingly optimistic-feeling place, and was a leading candidate for the setting of our new home. After a while, we concluded we were drawn to Shanklin because it reminded us of a miniature Southsea, where we had lived for many years. That, we both agreed, did not fit in with our tenet of doing and living somewhere completely different, which I guess is why we ended up where we have.

~

More than perhaps anywhere else on the Island, Sandown is a classic bucket-and-spade resort. Its sometimes gaudy and in-your-facedness is perhaps magnified, because it sits surrounded by an area of timeless natural beauty.

Like Shanklin, the town has long attracted visitors, some more welcome than others. With its wide, sweeping and flat bay, it was a natural landfall for raiding parties from the other side of the English Channel. In 1543 a castle to repel them was under construction when a French fleet arrived and was fought off after a long and bloody battle. Sandown castle was lost to the waves, then replaced with a number of Palmerstonian forts.

Like its nearest neighbour, the town grew in popularity as an upmarket resort in the 19th century. The safe bathing conditions were a particular attraction as the idea of immersing yourself in the sea became trendy. The royal seal of approval was given in the summer of 1874 when the Crown Prince of Germany and his wife, children and entourage rented a number of seafront properties and donned their bathing costumes.

Celebrities soon followed suit, and author Lewis Carroll and even the German Romantic composer Richard Strauss were to be seen taking the air on the promenade or splashing in the shallows.

It's not really clear when or why Sandown morphed from an upmarket spa to a relatively cheap and cheerful holiday destination, but nowadays it has much to offer. Apart from the sandy beaches and pier, there's a zoo, wildlife animal sanctuary, adventure playgrounds and a dinosaur museum. Along and above the prom there are kebab and fish and chip emporiums, pubs and cafes galore.

A recent and unique addition to the visitor attractions offering is the National Poo Museum. Exhibits include Prehistoric poo, faeces that look like a cereal bar, and the droppings of foxes, lions, a tawny owl and the Lesser Madagascan Tenrec.

At time of writing, entry was free but donations welcome. I contacted the proprietors and suggested I donate a small black bag containing the waste product of a famous local author, but my offer was politely refused.

On the dark side, there is evidence of deprivation, unemployment and the social ills that come with it. Ironically, the once-grand hotels of another age had become halls of residence for local homeless, though some haunts of Costa-del-Dole tourists are being replaced by budget hotels and plush prom-side apartment blocks.

The decline was inevitable as It has long been as cheap for families to chase the sun as holiday at home. But it's an ill wind, and the pandemic which is destroying so many holiday industries may just help revive Sandown's fortunes.

~

I have been trawling the internet for a French supplier who will export mole mines to non-EU countries. A friend in Carcassonne who knows of my problem said his neighbour evicted a persistent mole by simply blowing it up. He attached an advertisement for a device called a *détauper* - literally a 'de-moler' - which is legally available in France.

Basically, it is a tiny land mine which is set off when the mole passes nearby. My friend said his neighbour had overdone it and sown his garden with more than a dozen of the devices. The resulting chain reaction when one was set off by the mole did the trick but also turned his garden into a wasteland and totalled his conservatory.

~

I shall not tell my wife I am considering a more drastic deterrent to de-mole our garden, but, short of a professional mole catcher I have tried everything else.

On the advice of an Irish musician friend, I tried playing my penny whistle at dawn and dusk, but had to stop when it set all the dogs in the neighbourhood off in a barking and whining frenzy. The forest of bottles on sticks I tried had been contemptuously felled when I came into the garden the next morning. Thinking it might have been an exceptionally strong wind I put them back in place. Hours later Mr Mole had toppled them all again. To me, it seemed a casual demonstration of his view of my attempts to dislodge him.

Enraged, I got my wooden Breton sabots from the attic and spent hours clog-dancing my way across the slabs. It didn't affect the mole's excavations, but did amuse or bemuse a number of passing riders. Used to my behaviour, the lady instructor who caught me peeing on the badger holes in the fence didn't turn a hair and gave me the usual good morning. I made sure she was not passing when I funnelled about a gallon of my prototype urine-based mole repellent into Mr Moles underground highway.

I don't think I shall bother with the commercial bottling and launch of Mole-B-Gone as it has had the opposite effect than intended. As if in revenge at trying the stink bomb tactic, he has expanded his area of underground operations, and venturing anywhere in the back garden is like picking our way through a minefield.

~

One of the reasons we bought our new home was because of the lack of neighbours on one side for at least a mile. This has changed now a hopefully temporary resident has set up home in the woodlands next door.

I was pumping a final pint of my home-made mole deterrent into a new tunnel when I became aware of being watched, looked round and saw a distinctive figure leaning on the woodland side of our fence.

A lot of older men in the village have developed eccentric modes of dress and the growth of long hair and beard into almost an art form; my watcher would be a serious contender in any competition for Most Lifelike Worzel Gummidge.

He was a tall, almost gaunt man, wearing one of those once-fashionable Peruvian-style bobble hats, from which exploded a mass of ringleted, grey hair. A hugely bushy beard reached to his chest, revealing only broken-veined cheeks, a long, broken nose and small, oddly bright eyes. In a way, the effect was of a small mammal peering through a gap in a snow-coated hedge.

We looked at each other for a moment, then he removed a very slim roll-up cigarette from his mouth with a be-mittened hand, and observed in surprisingly mellifluous and cultured tones: 'That's a funny way to water a garden.'

I agreed and said it would be if I were, then explained the object of the exercise.

'Ah, he said, 'Moles are not welcome, then?'

I looked at his old army greatcoat and the two overflowing carrier bags he was resting on the fence and thought about saying he must know the feeling, but instead said 'I wouldn't mind if they weren't doing so much damage.'

He nodded gravely, then re-lit his stogie with a match which he carefully returned to the box. He drew deeply on it, then put the stub into matchbox, and asked: 'Have you tried anything else?'

'Apart from asking it nicely, rigging up wind chimes and sticking bottles on sticks around the place, no, I haven't.'

'Ah,' he said again, then: 'They say dog shit will do it.'

'I don't have a dog, I'm afraid.'

Appearing not to notice my testy tone, he waved a hand expansively towards the track and said: 'Plenty of it about, though.'

Unable to think of a suitable put-down, I turned back to the job in hand until he said:

'Or there's coffee grounds or dead fish, and they do say exhaust fumes will do it.'

'Bit of a job to get the car into the garden,' I said shortly. 'Anything less troublesome?'

He fingered his beard as if searching for any remnants of a previous meal, then said: 'Moles are haemophiliac, and some people put something sharp like rose cuttings, barbed wire or broken glass in the tunnels. Bit of a bugger if you find it with your fingers after Mr Mole has gone, though.'

I sat back on my heels and began to show interest. 'Any other old wives' tales?'

'They don't like creosote or sump oil, but it does make a mess of the garden.' He paused to examine his beard again, then continued: 'The French swear by marshmallow.'

'Are you serious?' I asked, interested in spite of myself.

'Absolutely.' The soup-strainer moustache moved as he smiled and revealed a gappy row of yellowing teeth. 'The idea is that the mole eats the marshmallow and it swells up and ...*pouf.*' He blew his cheeks out and made a gesture to indicate an exploding mole. 'Of course,' he continued, 'the moles being French, it has to be the most expensive marshmallow, hand-made from the finest ingredients.'

'And where do I get this beluga caviar level of marshmallow?' I asked.

He reached for his rustic cigarette case, then said: 'In France, presumably. But I suppose if all else fails you could try rubbing a dead mouse with a piece of copper money under a new moon while reciting the Hindu mantra for the Dead in reverse.'

'And what's that supposed to do?'

My new friend smoothed his moustache, looked thoughtful, gave his gappy smile again and said; 'No idea. I just made it up.'

Our new neighbour is called Will and he is a more than interesting character.

After I'd poured the remainder of the mole deterrent into the funnel, he invited me to his place for a cup of herbal tea. He saw me looking at the bulging carrier bags and said it was surprising what supermarkets threw out, but he had actually bought the tea bags.

He led me into the heart of the woods and I saw he had taken over a tepee of branches and an old tarpaulin put up by children. Given the drought, I was glad to see he used a small camping stove rather than naked fire to brew up.

Inside his wooden tent, a length of foam with a sleeping bag on top was laid out, and beside it a wind-up torch and a well-thumbed copy of the Anglo-Saxon epic poem, *Beowulf*. An old but obviously once top-of-the-range framed rucksack completed his belongings.

Over a shared plastic beaker of citrus ginger tea, Will told me it was his first visit to the Isle of Wight. He has read of the Island's pagan past and rich history, and plans to walk the coastal path, stopping off at burial mounds and prehistoric landmarks while the summer lasts. He is about half-way through his journey, and has been mostly sleeping in friendly farmers' barns. Sometimes he has bedded down in garages or sheds, mostly with the owners' permission. When his journey is complete, he will return to France, a country he has wandered around for more than forty years. This has been a summer break for him, and his peregrinations mean he knows of and is known at monasteries and foyers (hostels for passing vagrants) all around the country.

Now and then he will stay in an hotel when he is flush from selling an article about his exploits to British magazines. Every now and then he will receive a windfall from a charity looking after former writers who are down on their luck. He cheerily admits that when the weather is hard and he is broke and there are no foyers nearby, he will sometimes stay in hotels and leave without paying. If that happens, he makes amends by writing a glowing review of the hotel in his next article.

Again and with refreshing candour, he says that not being able to meet the bill for dinner and an overnight in a five-star hotel in the Loire valley is one of the reasons he is spending the summer here. Most of the hotels he bumps don't bother to make the effort to pursue him, but the Hotel Grande in Saumur would not be mollified by a flattering report and put the local *Gendarmerie* on his case.

When he learns of my interest and travels in France, he tells me that, of all the places he has travelled and lived in, he feels most at home there. He believes this to be so because they value culture and the arts more highly than money. Except, he says dismissively, the owners of large and vulgar hotels.

It's too early to ask how such an intelligent and clearly erudite man came to be in his situation, but I think it will be a story to which it will be well worth listening.

~

'No, and don't even think about it.'

'About what?'

'Inviting your new mate to move in with us.'

I looked hurt. 'What makes you think I was going to suggest that?'

My wife sighed. 'How long have we been married?'

'But it's only for a few days...or so.'

'Bad enough to have one man with dubious hygiene standards on the premises', she retorted. 'You really expect me to turn my house into a home for smelly old hobos?'

'He's not a hobo,' I protested mildly, 'just a bloke who likes to wander round France. Loads of people do that every year.'

'Yes, but they're called tourists and they pay for the pleasure.'

I tried another tack: 'He can sleep and eat in the summerhouse and he uses the sports centre for his ablutions. He won't ever need to come into the house.'

I let her think about that, then came in with the clincher. 'He's very good at gardening - and getting rid of moles, and he could do other stuff on the house, and then there's the painting. He'd be brilliant for that.'

She frowned, but I could see she was softening. 'Who says we want the fence painting?'

'Not that sort of painting; I mean *your* sort of painting. You must admit he's got a great face for a portrait. I reckon you could win a prize with a picture of him, and you'd have a free sitter.'

~

Will is, for the moment, home and dry.

I deliberately waited till it was raining and then showed my wife his leaky den in the woodlands. Her feminine compassion kicked in and she said she would make up the sofa bed in the summerhouse. On the way back along the track she warned me that he had better not get too comfortable, but in the last week he has more than earned his keep.

He is currently doing double-digging and weeding in the allotment, while Donella is working on her painting of him in her studio. When they discussed the project, he said he would be quite happy to pose nude for a Life study, but would prefer to keep his socks on as his circulation was not what it was. She said thanks but no thanks and that she would be happy with a head and shoulders study.

I am on a bench in a favourite spot by the fort on top of Golden Hill. The local buzzard is sitting on a tree, watching owl-like as two men make an intricate and inventive maze of willow branches. Far below, a skiff is skimming along the Yar, and from this distance looks remarkably like a water boatman.

I'm on the first leg of a round trip of five miles that will take me from Golden Hill along the coast to The Needles, and past several historic landmarks. Best of all it will only cross one road. I take a deep breath and nod goodbye to the buzzard.

It's not rural France, but this part of the rough diamond comes a pretty close runner-up.

~

My new amanuensis is sitting comfortably immobile in a deckchair in the summerhouse, a drooping roll-up hanging from his lips as Donella puts the finishing touches to his portrait.

'Hello darling,' she says, looking up, '- as the man said to the horse, why the long face?'

'I just got a call from the agency,' I say morosely.

'Ah,' she says, laying her brush down. 'Good news?'

'Not really,' I say. 'I didn't get the part.'

Will murmurs sympathetically and my wife tries to look surprised.

'Never mind,' she says brightly, 'There's always the extra work.'

'Not yet,' I say, 'they want me to test for two other parts. They say they like the look of my face.'

'Well.' My wife says, walking over to the fridge and the bottle of Loire Rosé I know she has been keeping for a good news day. 'that's more than can be said for poor old Ollie Reed.'

12

"The wold dooman ded clapperclaa 'en proper."
("The old woman did scratch his face well.")

From *A Dictionary of the Isle of Wight Dialect and Provincialisms Used in the Island*, compiled by William Long

Summer is on the wing, and we are approaching, as Tennyson influencer John Keats had it, the season of mists and mellow fruitfulness. The days grow shorter, but the sun smiles, the sea sparkles and it seems more Isle of Capri than Isle of Wight.

The continuing heatwave also means an extension to the official shorts-wearing season, and has given me another fund-raising scheme to help meet the potential cost of anchoring our home in permanent place.

Perhaps it's being half-Scottish (and perhaps it's my bottom half) but I've always envied women that they have the choice of how to show or conceal their legs. They may choose trousers or skirt or dress or even ball gown when it suits them and the situation. Unless in transition, most blokes have a choice of long or short trousers. There's the kilt for Scots and Welshmen, but then there's all the expense and kit and caboodle that goes with it. From a gardening perspective, I suppose a sporran would be good for holding small garden tools and you could keep your pruning knife in your sock, but it could be dodgy when bending down anywhere near a nettle patch or a thorny fruit plant. Also, a real kilt can be as pricey as any designer frock.

I suppose there's always the option of buying a double-x size summer dress from the local charity shop for working in the allotment and gardens, but I don't think it would go with my beard.

Having thought about it, I believe I've come up with a corker of invention which combines the economy of a pair of cut down trousers with the efficacy of a kilt or skirt. I have simply threaded lengths of springy wire through the bottom of each leg of my favourite shorts. It keeps them rigidly circular and away from clammy contact with the thighs, and allows greatly increased air circulation.

Before taking the big step of applying for a patent I modelled them for my wife, who was not enthusiastic. She said they made me look even more ridiculous than usual, and had I not thought of what would happen when I sat down in mixed company? My invention might increase ventilation, but it could also expose me to serious charges if I sat down with my shorts pointing at a passing female. I should know how much journalists love alliteration, and *Fairly Famous Author Fined for Flashing* would be a gift.

I saw her point and agreed to return my shorts to a wire-less state, but did not start a row by reminding her that there is no such thing as bad publicity.

~

The heat continues, and unless watered at least twice a day the gaping fissures on our allotment plot threaten to swallow whole rows of produce. I am not sure if the lack of water has been good or bad for the foundations of our home, but hopefully the house and garage have settled down and got over their apparently magnetic attraction.

In the gardens, our soft fruits grow ever more plumptious. In particular it should be a bumper year for our Breton vines, the darkly glowing grapes of which will be pressed into the first bottling of Chateau Greenbanks.

The closest the Island comes to the rest of Great Britain:
Hurst Castle

Sadly, this time of year is also a time of partings, and the swallows, wheatears and warblers have flown south.

Gladly, and whether because of my whistle playing or the malodorous effect of my widdle or the threat of mining his bunker, Mr Mole has moved on. I suspect he will return when the earthworm population in our garden has recovered and the stink subsided.

A most unwelcome departure came when Will packed his haversack and carrier bags and left us.

He refused our offer of a lift to the ferry port, but did accept our small gifts of a large meat pie, a dozen fairy ferry port cakes and an apple crumble from my wife. I gave him a hand-carved Breton staff, and he said he would think of me when he used it to fight off creditors or any *gendarmes* intent on his arrest.

We shook hands and embraced in the French way at the garden gate, then watched as he walked briskly down the track. He did not look back, but raised his new staff in salute as he turned the corner and was gone. We walked back to the summerhouse and I thought how I will miss him and the aroma of his roll-up cigarettes and even his socks. He was only with us for a fortnight, but we both feel the loss and had grown fond of him. He was a cultured, erudite and articulate man, with whom we shared a love of France. He was also a true philosopher and in all the stories he told of his wanderings, he never complained about the bad days and experiences. One night when he had had an extra glass of Sancerre, he looked into his glass reflectively and said how much he envied my wife and I our togetherness. But, he said, holding out the empty glass, we all choose the path we take and must stick with it.

Donella blew her nose loudly as he went out of sight and out of our lives, and I thought how I envied and sympathised with him at the same time. Will is truly free, but has to pay the price and put up with hard commons at times. I also think he may be constantly on the move to get away from his past, or even himself.

~

I'll miss our long, lazy evenings sitting outside the summerhouse while swapping stories of our small adventures in France. I'll also miss working with Will on my audition videos for the thriller to be filmed on the Island.

In our rehearsals, he would run me through my lines, direct my movements and expressions, then film and edit the short sequences. It was obvious how familiar and adept he was with that sort of work, and he did let a few names slip which made me think he had been involved at a high level in television programme production.

They say you can find anyone if you look in the right places on the World Wide Web, and it did not take long to find our recent guest.

Along with university friends who went on to become household names in the arts, Will was certainly a noted figure in radio and television as the Swinging Sixties drew to a close. On You Tube I found a series of TV documentaries about authors and artists which he had presented and produced.

He was young and very handsome. I then searched

for anything with his name attached to it, and followed his life as he married and had children and climbed the media greasy pole. Then came an article in a snidey satire magazine about how he had come home and found his wife in bed with a friend. Will had walked out, leaving house, family and friends and work and gone on the road in France.

I sat on the terrace and wondered where he was and if he had found a bed for the night in Limoges or Avignon or Chartres, and how different his life had turned out from the dazzling careers of his starry university friends.

Along with debating how many angels could be squeezed on the head of a pin, philosophers have for millennia argued for Fate or self-determination ruling our futures. I am still undecided, but suspect that Will ended up getting what he wanted, even if he did not want it. At least, that somehow makes his story less sad.

~

The lady from the agency called to say how good my new audition tape was compared with the first one, and asked if I had had professional help. I didn't like to say it had been produced by a passing tramp, so said I was a quick learner. She said there had been no reaction from the casting agency, but she would let me know as soon as she heard from them.

I told Donella about the call over dinner, and she said she hoped I would not be too disappointed if it all came to nothing. When I thanked her sarcastically for her enthusiasm and confidence she reached across the table and squeezed my hand and said she was sure I could see how unlikely it was that the agency whose key figures were probably of an age with our oldest grandson would be unlikely to pick someone of my age for the part of a serving police officer. I retorted that they could do wonders nowadays with make-up and electronic wizardry and exampled how they had made Robert de Niro and Joe Pesci look forty years younger for flashbacks in a recent gangster movie. She smiled and agreed but said the budget for a modest TV drama probably would not stretch to that sort of post-production trickery. She also reminded me that if it did happen, I would be the oldest police sergeant to appear on TV screens since Jack Warner in *Dixon of Dock Green*. And that he was only sixty years of age when the series was launched.

~

Life goes on as normally as it can in these strange times.

Although or perhaps because we are in the lowest category for infection rates, I detect an air of uneasiness on the streets. Freshwater is used to visitors and makes good money from them, but nowadays for some villagers an unfamiliar face can be a cause for concern. There's no open hostility, just the way that some of the older locals make a point of crossing the road or make sure their face masks are securely in place when a stranger appears. It must have been a little like that in villages at the time of the Black Death.

Regardless of visitor numbers, the trendification of Freshwater gathers pace.

A lot of money has obviously been spent on the abandoned building alongside the Red Cross charity shop, and it has transmogrified into a boutique (code for 'small') hotel.

Even more a subject for local debate, the latest edition of the parish council newsletter has announced that the elderly public toilets are to be demolished and a task force been tasked to come up with a suitable replacement. Predictably, the response in the on-line village forum has been less than enthusiastic. One poster forecast that the new loo would doubtless be a windowless, claustrophobic, unisex, gender-neutral facility with, worst of all, an entry fee. He personally found the current set-up completely satisfactory, as he used the old toilets for a pee and the hotel in Freshwater Bay for a poo. Both, he added, were free.

Another change that is a small personal blow is that our favourite bookshop is to be upcycled.

Where we once sat in a higgle-piggle of dusty but comfortingly aromatic old books while a slow but kindly old lady served tea in fine if mismatching porcelain cups, will soon become an outlet for locally-made truffles, bonbons, vegan lemon cake and luxury continental chocolates.

Next door in the Arts and Crafts Cooperative, you can now pick up a bamboo toothbrush or silk and linen eye mask with lavender and linseed. I am told they are known to be a perfect relaxant after a yoga session and a snip at ten quid.

As with dog owners and beard-wearers but unlike Jedi Knights, I can find no reliable data as to how many thatched properties relative to population density are to be found on the Island. In our village we even have a thatched church, for God's sake.

Whatever the facts, I'd have a modest wager that the Isle of Wight sits towards the top of any national census of the variety and number of buildings topped with straw rather than slate or tiles.

There's something about the word 'cottage'* which summons up a cosy nest of rugged whitewashed walls, wood-burning stove and, of course, an Aga cooker. If it's got a thatch and an appealing nameplate next to the roses round the front door you can add a hundred grand or so on the asking price, even in this land of plenty.

It is of course the imagery rather than the reality which adds to the appeal, but it was not always so.

Available vegetation is the oldest form of roof-covering, and straw or reeds were the most available materials for country dwellers until the late 1800s. Slate was becoming more commercially available and the canal and railway system gave it passage to the countryside.

So, a slate roof became a status symbol and had real snob appeal over a thatch, a perception which has of course completely reversed over fairly recent years.

We briefly occupied a 15th-century thatched cottage with all the trendy accessories like three-foot-thick walls, flagged floors and terminal dry rot in the massive ceiling beams. It was an interesting time, but we soon learned there is a price to pay for living in a chocolate box. To start with there's the constant fear that a wind-borne spark from a neighbour's bonfire could literally bring the house down. Then there was the damp running up the walls as well as down, and the wind whistling through the Grade Two-protected windows. It was nice to be asked by passing tourists if we would take a photo of them outside our lovely home, but not so nice when the rats were playing kiss-chase overhead.

There are two more-or-less direct routes from West Wight to Newport. Those who prefer a slow and scenic drive will take the Yarmouth coastal road.

Bus, lorry and ambulance drivers in a hurry and lunatics usually take what locals call the Middle Road. Curiously, it's also a favourite route for arse-in-the-air cyclists who like to ride side-by-side at twenty miles an hour as they chat about past

excursions, future plans and the joys of creating long tailbacks.

~

Calbourne is an ancient village which demonstrates perfectly the way a busy through-road can divide a community, while a lane can make it a much, much nicer place to live.

The much-used road must be a good site for a passing-trade pub, car sales lot and ancient water-mill-tuned-theme park, and The Middle Way has all three on and near the Calbourne crossroads. But I don't think many people would like to live yards from where hurtling behemoths and boy racers pass.

The contrast makes turning off the Mad Max highway and into the village (cliché alert) like going back in time and another world. In the peaceful and very pleasant Calbourne, there's an adequacy of interesting thatched cottages, a village green complete with a cricket team, and a delightfully solid-looking Norman church with its origins in the 9th century.

All Saints sits amidst a sea of mostly ancient gravestones, and inside there's a Victorian organ and a brass depiction of a recumbent knight in full armour, hands set in prayer and dog beneath his feet. The image is of William Montagu, accidently slain by his father the Earl of Salisbury in 1379 during a joust. It may have been my imagination, but he does seem to wear a surprised and even hurt look. For sure, for anyone with a smidgeon of sensitivity, to stand in this ancient and serene bubble is to connect with history.

Back in the present, and anyone irritated by the noise and intrusion of the latest must-have gadgets would be pleased to note the sign on the gate to the recreation ground. By order of the parish council, comes the stern admonition, 'drone devices' as well as dogs are prohibited from entry. Going by the tone, and had drones been around a couple of centuries ago, I can imagine the punishment for breaking the canon might be the clipping of an ear or at least a spell in the village stocks.

~

Just across the lane and at the end of a winding driveway past the octagonal gatehouse is a privately-owned manor house which dates back to the reign of Edward the Confessor. Next to the gatehouse is the entry to a real visitor magnet, and a quirky row of houses which appealed to royalty, landscape painters and poets across the centuries.

Apparently designed by someone with a vision of the future and what would look really good on picture-postcards, Winkle Street is a terrace of 18th century stone houses, overlooking the village stream and open fields beyond. The 'Caul Bourne' waterway runs clear and fast and the remains of an ancient sheep dip are still on view.

There are several proposals as to the origin of the unusual name of the short street. My least favourite is that 'winkle' used to have the same meaning as 'to twinkle'. A more sustainable suggestion is that the word was also used to describe a lane which turned a corner and led to nowhere, like the shell of the mollusc. Best of all for me is that, in Victorian times, the villagers used to make regular horse and cart trips to gather winkles from the shore at Newtown. I like to think of those residents now resting in the churchyard going a-winkling on a pleasant day. Nowadays, Newtown is only a few minutes away along the Middle Road, but in those days it would have seemed like a long and rewarding day trip to the seaside.

~

I take my ease beside the ancient sheep dip and think about what it would actually be like to live here if we could afford the prices. A quick search on my phone and I am more than surprised to discover that the imposing five-bedroom end-of-terrace Georgian house I have been admiring is on sale and valued at not a deal more than our boring bungalow and terminally-ill garage.

Perhaps people don't like to be stared at through the window by rubber-neckers, or the bargain price may be because it is a Grade II listed property, the ownership of which means observing all the regulations and undertaking the inevitably costly maintenance, but even so I know where I would rather live.

~

Walking back up to the main road, I spot a plaque on a sturdy stone cottage and squint over the wall to find out who or what it records. To my delight, I find it is the birthplace in 1839 of the Island's very own Dr Johnson.

Son of a farming family and Author of a *Dictionary of the Isle of Wight Dialect and Provincialisms Used in the Island*, W. H. Long pursued a literary career and became a writer and antiquarian. Along with the dictionary and other works, he compiled more than fifty songs 'from the mouths of the peasantry.'

Almost hugging myself with delight, I leave this lovely, peaceful place and head for the noise and danger of the Middle Road.

It's claimed that Calbourne is arguably the prettiest village in the Island. I think that would start a few arguments, but it is, I reckon, definitely in the running.

~

My phone rings as I reach the car.

I look at the number and my heart gives a little hiccup. It is my agent.

We greet each other and she says something that is lost to me as a huge liquid cement-bearing lorry trundles by.

'I'm sorry,' I shout, '…can you repeat that?'

'I said I just heard from the casting agency.'

She says something else, her words again drowned out, this time by the number 7 bus from Newport. It is not being held up by cyclists, stray sheep or aged drivers, so is batting along at a good pace and the leaves on the bay hedge behind me flutter in the slipstream.

'So sorry,' I yell again, 'can you say that again?'

'Of course.' She raises her voice and shouts down the line: 'I said "congratulations." You've got the part. You're going to be Sergeant Westfield.'

*The word 'cottage' is said to have originated in England in the Middle Ages. A peasant farmer was a 'cotter', so the place he lived in was a cottage. The roots are said to stretch even further back to Old French and the Norse 'kot' for 'hut', but let's not get into the semantics.

Speaking in Tongues

When you think about it, it's truly remarkable how many varieties of local dialect, accent and argot you can hear in our tiny country. The mix of high-pitched west country whine and Sarf London glottal - T stoppage in my home city of Portsmuff is a fine example. Given the Isle of Wight's apartness from the mainland and the locals' alleged reluctance to go *athert* (see below), I was surprised to find I could detect no distinctive Isle of Wight accent or dialect. That was not always so, as these examples from W H Long's Dictionary illustrate:

"That ere wut rick is all of a hoogh."
("That oat rick is well out of shape.")

"Be you gwyne athert to-day?"
("Are you going over the water to day?")

"He auverdrode the waggon gwyne down the shoot."
("He upset the waggon going down the hill.")

"That's a bonnygoo hoss o'yourn, varmer."
(That's a spirited horse you have, farmer.")

"Wull ye hay zomethin to yet? But there, we onny got a vew brocks left from dinnertime to offer ye."
"(Will you have something to eat? But we have only a few fragments left from dinner to offer you.")

"I've ben and cagged en now, I louz."
("I have offended him now, I think.")

"The wold man sims terbul crousty this mornen."
("The old man is very ill-tempered this morning.")

"I'll gi'thee a dack wi'the prongsteel if thee doesn't mind."
("I'll give you a blow with the prong handle if you don't take care.")

N.B. I don't know if J. K. Rowling ever came here, but there is something very Harry Potter-ish about some aspects of the Isle of Wight. Strange and magical place and lane names abound, and it is interesting that the local name for a bumblebee is the same as that of the headmaster of Hogwarts school of Witchcraft and Wizardry, one Albus Dumbledore…

∞∞∞∞

13

As well as one of the oldest populations in the UK, the Isle of Wight has the oldest theme park in the UK (and perhaps the world) at Blackgang Chine and the oldest telephone box, sited at Bembridge. For those interested, it is of the K1 classification, erected in 1921 and still not vandalised.

*When running through the final proofing, I noticed that I had unintentionally written 'oddest' rather than 'oldest' here. Presumably, the editor had not thought it a simple typo and was quite happy to leave it in place.

'There's about a ton of lead stinking of incense in the loft. The owner says he don't remember who he bought it from. Yeah, *right...*'

My dialogue coach does not respond, but an elderly lady scoops up her bulbous-eyed rat of a dog and scurries past, eyes above her mask pointedly averted.

She thinks I am talking to the life-size carving of an Edwardian soldier sitting on the bench next to me. In fact, as I am tempted to call out after her, I am merely an actor rehearsing his lines in a suitably secluded place.

Things have moved quickly since I was offered both the parts I auditioned for in the thriller to be shot on the Island. According to my agent, the series' producers must be impressed with my video, as they are going to roll both roles into one. The good news is that I will get paid more; the slightly scary news is that I will have to learn twice as many lines. There are only four sentences and twenty-seven words in total, but the task of delivering them on camera is assuming the significance of Hamlet's soliloquy.

One of the problems is that I am used to reading from a script when appearing (or rather not appearing) on radio; for my TV appearances as a presenter, I have always been speaking my own words. I'm also no longer as young as I was. Sometimes it's hard enough to remember what you went into a room for by the time you arrive.

Another problem is that, in real life I probably utter ten thousand words a day (my wife would say that is a severe underestimate) but now I have to learn to say words that have literally been put in my mouth by someone else. And I have to say them as if they are mine, and say them naturally. As Donella said when I told her my problem, that is what actors do.

Perhaps the biggest problem is having nobody who understands acting to work with. Will is somewhere in France, and I assume Mary next door has had little experience in drama coaching. She is also profoundly deaf and I notice she has taken to turning off or removing her hearing aids when I call in to keep her company with a chat. The obvious partner to work with is my wife, but when we had a run-through and I asked her to be brutally honest about my performance, she was.

That's why I'm sitting on this bench, practicing my lines on my unresponsive companion. He may not be able to give me any constructive criticism, but at least he will not tell me how wooden my performance is.

Most people would be more than happy to have one country park on their doorstep; we have two. Golden Hill starts outside our back gate, while the Victoria country park sits on the shore a mile away by the scenic route.

Henry VIII built a fort at Sconce Point to guard the Needles Approach in 1545. It was replaced by Fort Victoria in 1850, and took the form of a brick-built triangle with two seaward-facing batteries. Though never having to take on invaders, the fort was used as a training base in both world wars and was finally decommissioned in 1962.

Instead of barrack rooms and gun emplacements, the old building offers an excellent café and the sort of tourist attractions that help make the Isle of Wight the delightfully quirky place can be. Where else

Named for Victoria's consort: Fort Albert

would you find small but excellent private enterprises like a reptilarium, planetarium and a very,
very big miniature railway layout?

On the sea side of the fort are views of the Solent

and passing craft. There are cannons to play on and the shore to search for unusual shells and even fossils. Shark and crocodile teeth are not common, but findable.

From here, Milford-on-sea and its tapas bars, bookshops and bakers and gastro-pubs sit no more than a mile or so across the Solent, but occupies a different world.

Mainland property prices obviously start from the shoreline. A beach hut at Colwell Bay on our side of the great divide will set you back around seventeen thousand pounds. The asking price for a three-metre-square hut on an identical beach at Milford will cost you coming up for £30,000.

~

A maze of tracks and paths lead from the fort and through the Queen Victoria Country Park, and alongside them are examples of how inventive the human mind can be when given a lump of wood and a sharp tool or two. Examples along the way include branches which have become serpents, forked of tongue and beady of eye. There are also wooden butterflies, dinosaurs and even fantastic dragons, some so realistic they look as if they lived and roared fire before being petrified by a wave of a Potteresque wand.

Of particular fascination is a tree stump, the rings marking momentous events over hundreds of years. The innermost ring shows it as a sapling at the time of the French Revolution, and its growth witnessed the Battle of Trafalgar and two World Wars. It is a simple but striking way of showing how near and far history can be. Also for young explorers, there are virulently green stew ponds and apparently impenetrable undergrowth where mythical beasts may still lurk.

For older ramblers, there is more than a sufficiency of benches and chairs hewn from stumps, and it is on one that my drama coach sits and watches time go by.

Apart from the obvious nominees like telephones and television, zip fasteners, Viagra and pop tarts, any list of the simplest yet greatest inventions of the past two hundred years would have to include the electrical bicycle.

Although it has only been accepted as socially acceptable and even cool in recent times, a patent for a bike that did the hard work for you was taken out by one Ogden Bolton jnr in 1895. Two years later Mr Hosiah W Libbey came up with a proposal for a bike with two motors. One was for riding on the flat, the other came into play when the going got tough.

My dad always said that timing was the secret of success...or lack of it. It certainly proved to be so with the electric bicycle, because, despite constant improvements and innovations they were eclipsed by the popularity of the motor car.

The e-bike was a sight rare enough to cause comment until well into the new Millennium, and people still sniff and say 'cheating, eh?' when they see the battery clamped to the framework of my old machine.

The fact is that battery power does not replace muscle power, it enhances it. My e-bike has three settings that can miraculously shear the years off my legs and lungs. In first gear, I can pedal briskly along as if a healthy teenager. When there's an upward slope ahead, I can switch to second or third gear depending on how steep it is and how much help I need to get up it. In a place like the Isle of Wight, I would be able to get no further than the end of the road with a standard do-it-all-yourself machine. Now my wife and I can glide up hill and down dale and think little of covering thirty miles a day.

Best of all for me is overtaking some lairy lycra-clad show-off puffing and straining up a steep rise and giving him an encouraging wave and patronising smile as I pass.

~

It may be healthier to cycle rather than drive, but it can also be a lot more dangerous.

Today, we pedalled our way along the coastal road and in couple of miles experienced three near-death experiences.

Throwing unheard protests in their wake, I try to understand the thinking or mentality of those drivers who brush by us within inches, or rush to squeeze through the diminishing gap when a ten-ton cement lorry is coming the other way.

To be charitable, it may be that the drivers who put us in fear of our lives have never ridden a bike and don't know how scary it is to have half a ton of metal speeding by inches from your kneecap. A more worrying option is that they are so incompetent they cannot judge how close they are coming. Or, perhaps like the careless cyclists we encounter off-road, they just don't care.

~

Sometimes I wonder if, like the commonplaceness of dolphins, sharks, fossils and ghosts, the alleged arrival of sea eagles on the Island is all part of the tourist board's drive to increase visitor numbers.

The top-of-the-range squirrel food lies untroubled in the feeding box on the fence. I'm occasionally alerted by walkers on Golden Hill that they have just seen one, but it has always disappeared by the time I get to its last sighting place. It is the same with the sea eagles; I have returned to Newtown at least a dozen times since my first visit, and each time I have just missed a sighting.

On the way back from a fruitless hour in the hide,

we met a weather-beaten lady with a small dog at her heels. When we learned she was a genuine, time-served caulkhead, I asked if she had seen or heard of any visits. She looked thoughtful and then said I had just missed it, as if the bird was the number seven bus to Newport.

Rather than take on the coastal road again and risk rage and limb if not life, we are on a leisurely ride home through the green and pleasant heart of West Wight.

It would be wrong to say that, alongside the winding lanes past fields of sheep and cows, the villages remain unchanged. But ignore the parked cars and satellite dishes and the occasional newbuild and you could indeed be in another age. This illusion must occur in pockets elsewhere in the country; it just seems so much more so here on the Island.

Almost joined at the hip, even the names of Thorley and Wellow seem made to go together. Just say them together and try not to adopt a west country burr.

These are villages that have been around for a long time, and seem to like being what and where they are. At Thorley, there's a manor house that was around long before the Normans arrived, and a fine 13th century church. Just up the road at Wellow, a nicely distressed chapel has for the moment escaped inevitable conversion. The Women's Literary Institute is housed in a proper village hall with arched door and heavy-set clock above. Round the corner is the thatched post office as was, and the notice board tells of waltz and zumba dance sessions, art clubs and meetings to protest about a plan to build another tranche of mostly unwanted new homes. A mark of the affability of these communities is how the bus shelters are stocked with books for those who need to escape the rain or sit and wait or are just having a night out. This is also very much not second-home territory, but real, living villages with old people pottering in their neat little gardens and children playing carelessly in the lanes.

We are resting in the churchyard, surrounded by gravestones, their sombre dignity emphasised by the sea of brightly coloured wild flowers in which they float. The occasional car putters by as if aware of the tranquillity of this spot and loath to rupture it. Over the flint wall at our backs a field is busy with a legion of free-range hens, overseen by possessively strutting cocks. Butterflies flutter and midges maraud. Bumble bees do what they do best, and their somnolent buzz is the quintessence of late summer.

We sit back and take tea and buns and wonder how it would be to live in a place like this. I suspect a lot of people would think they would like it until they tried.

Young people and those who must be stimulated by noise and chaos, would, of course, hate it here.

Another unknowable statistic, but I reckon the country-dwellers of the Isle of Wight must run more roadside enterprises than anywhere on the main-land.

You cannot drive through a village or hamlet without multiple invitations to stop and buy plants, plaster gnomes, bird nesting boxes, hand-wrought garden furniture, unwanted pets or children, home-grown veg and fruit or cakes. Houses on the mainland have restored bicycles or cars to flog at their gates. Here, horse shit is a common and popular commodity with a going rate of fifty pence a bag.

Most of all, though, it's eggs. Duck, goose but overwhelmingly chicken. A visiting Martian with a sketchy knowledge of our species might think that the improvised stalls with their home-made signs and honesty boxes could be roadside shrines.

It is possible that all these back gardens house a clutch of hens, but I wonder if some of the vendors might be doing trade with the owners of commercial collections of hens.

Seeing the displays reminds me of my dear mother and her love of hands-on, cash-only trading. She stayed often at my brother's thatched farmhouse in the Hampshire countryside and made considerably more than pin money by selling eggs and fruit and vegetables at the gate. She didn't need the extra income, but could not resist the trading opportunity.

When I mentioned that brother John did not keep hens or raise vegetables, she conceded that the allegedly home-grown produce had come from the shelves of the local Tesco. There was no harm in the small deception, and people always said it was worth paying a few pence more for so much more taste. If you thought about it, she said with a straight face, she was actually enhancing the pleasure of townspeople's drives in the countryside.

She had, she told me, first learned the benefits of selling at the garden gate in the early post-War years. Times then were hard and, she tartly reminded me, the extra income helped provide little luxuries. There was a problem with the little lion stamped on every eggshell bought from a shop or store in those days, but she got over it with the judicious application of just a smear of chicken poo. If anything, she said, it made the eggs look fresher and even more desirable.

~

The squirrel diner is proving popular, but to the wrong sort of customer. Some people call squirrels tree-rats, and our box is attracting a real one.

Hearing Donella's excited shout the other day, I joined her in the kitchen to see a furry creature with a long scaly tail gnawing away at the hinged lid of the feeder.

'Can't you explain how to open it,' my wife asked. 'It's obviously a squirrel of very limited intelligence.'

'Unless it's the only grey squirrel on the Island,' I said tactfully, it's technically a rat.'

~

We are in a quandary with Ratty.

My wife is fine with most of God's creatures unless they bite or sting or have eight legs. Woodlice regularly trek across the sitting-room floor without let or hindrance. Snails and even slugs are not a problem unless they threaten our crops. She normally has no quarrel with rats, and we quite amicably shared a mill cottage in Normandy with an extended family. They quite liked *EastEnders*, and would rush out of the wainscoting and line up in front of the television when the signature tune wailed out. Their favourite TV snack was Cheesy Whatsits or Marmite on toast, I remember.

As my wife says, the rat is at least putting the squirrel box to good use. He's not dexterous or clever enough to open the lid, but has, in the way of rats, gnawed his way in. Unsurprisingly he has become a regular customer and begun to bring his family and friends with him.

The problem is that the increasingly long line of eager diners flitting across the garden has not gone unnoticed. We think that Ratty & Co have a home on the allotment and enter our garden from next door. They have been seen, and Mary-next-door is not as much of an animal lover as my wife.

It has reached the point that something must be done. I have suggested capturing the Rat family and spray-painting them a shade of Crown Russet Red. Then we could pretend it was a family of red squirrels on their way to lunch.

Donella does not see that as a practical solution, and says something must be done before we get a visit from the Council Pest Control Team.

~

Despite hearing the good news from my agent, I had still somehow thought that my landing a part in the new TV drama was an elaborate hoax or a dream from which I would wake. The photos and audition videos showed me as I look to others, and in this youth-obsessed time, who was going to employ an actor thirty years older than the retiring age for the character he was portraying?

But confirmation that I had not imagined it all

arrived with a bulky package this morning, The postman looked a little bemused when I tried to give him a tip and made a performance of puzzling over what he had brought before saying: 'Ah, of course, it must be from my agent. It'll be the contract for my next role…'

In the kitchen, I tore the package open, and found the contract on top of a forest of other papers. I showed the terms of engagement to my wife, who looked at the bottom line and whistled appreciatively. I know she had been pleased for me when I landed the part, but had not wanted me to get too excited about establishing an extra income stream. Her attitude changed when she worked out that I will be paid more for three days filming than from six months of book-writing.

~

I had not realised there was so much more to this acting game than remembering one's lines and not walking into the furniture.

After signing and sending off the contract, I went through all the other documents. My bowels clenched when I saw the ocean of words to be rehearsed and remembered, then realised that as well as my lines I'd been sent everyone else's in every scene of every episode.

Then there were what they called the shooting scripts, the outside locations and schedules, each with precise notes of when and where I will be wanted. There were also separate call sheets and call times and more mysterious terms like 'bump', which, I discovered, is a one-off payment for extra work.

When I asked my agent what DC meant, she said it was trade-talk for dropping cues, forgetting my lines or when to come in. Ominously, she added that the director is known to be really fussy that 'his' actors stick to the script and don't ad-lib. I said I would do my best to be word-perfect, though I had heard that even really experienced performers used cue sheets. I had even read that while playing the title role in *The Godfather*, Marlon Brando never bothered to learn his lines and had them scattered around the set and even stuck on the foreheads and shirt fronts of actors with their backs to the camera.

My agent said she had heard those stories, but as I was not quite as established a star as Brando it might be best to make sure I learned and remembered my seven lines.

I said I would, but couldn't help thinking that perhaps the lack of lines might, perversely, be a problem. I know from voicing radio and TV commercials can mean over-concentration on stress and pitch and delivery of individual words. I once had to say the word 'nice' about a chocolate bar two dozen times before I and the producer were happy with it. A worrying example of this syndrome occurs in a Mike Leigh play-within-a-play in which the central character is an extra who is given a simple line of dialogue. He spends the weeks leading up to his appearance practicing over and over the single line, and inevitably gets it all wrong when at last in front of the camera. For some reason I can't banish the moment of terror and tragedy from my mind.

Europe had its wine lakes and cheese mountains; I have a fruit and veg Matterhorn.

Despite my best intentions, history repeats itself

and my massive surfeit of courgettes and tomatoes and runner beans repeats itself Groundhog Day-style every year. I know what is to come, yet cannot mend my ways and change what is to come.

It's no good trying to foist surplus off on fellow

allotmenteers, and they have begun to dive for cover when I approach with a sack of baby marrows. I've tried leaving stuff on the mutual path outside our patch, but when I return next day it will still be there. Sometimes the pile will have been augmented by other growers' surpluses.

I have tried leaving trays outside the supermarkets or putting them in the free food boxes inside, but they only like customers to donate things they have bought on the premises.

But this year I have taken steps to ensure that next year will be different. One of my near-neighbours is a lady of very mature years and almost infinite knowledge of the growing game. It is a fact that Greenfingers Gloria has been coaxing award-winning fruits and vegetables from the earth longer than many of our allotmenteers have been alive. There seems nothing she does not know about making the most of the soil and persuading pests to move on. There is a spring and summer pilgrimage to her old shed to rival the *Santiago de Compostela*, and some of the advice-seekers come from other allotments. One man is even said to catch the boat from the mainland whenever he is having problems with the size and shape of his competition entries.

The first step in my scheme to break my addiction to sowing much, much more than I need to reap was to hand over all the dozens of unopened and part-used seed packets to Gloria, while pledging not to go within ten yards of any garden centre display or catalogue during sowing time. When the time comes next year, she will dole out a sensible number of seeds in each category, and stand over me while I sow them.

I will try to keep to my promises and intents, but have already started stowing packet of alfalfa and white carrot seeds around the house in unlikely locations. This is because my wife is in cahoots with Greenfingers Gloria, and both are determined to break my addiction and save the potholders and people of Freshwater from my unwanted attentions.

~

A day riven with guilt as I prepared to commit murder.

It was with a heavy heart I went to the village hardware store and bought a tin of rat poison. The innocent-looking blue block was, the assistant assured me, effective and painless. The victim would feel nothing and there was a delayed effect, which meant it would die in its own home, perhaps surrounded by its loving family. I thought about asking how he could know it was painless, but understood he was only trying to make it easier for me to commit ratticide. When I asked how the poison was best employed, he said his way was to wrap a chunk of the recommended size in a piece of bacon or piece of cheese. If I wanted to give them an even more special last meal, chunks of a Mars bar would be highly appreciated and help the medicine go down.

~

I have been on death watch.

Donella was concerned that our red squirrel might appear and yaffle up the slices of deadly Mars bar, so I was detailed to hide in a nearby bush and make sure there were no tragic mistakes.

It was all I could do not to shout a warning as Ratty sped up the post. The box was emptied in moments and the doomed creature disappeared down the tunnel next to the garden shed.

I sat and thought how strange it is that we find squirrels and hedgehogs so cute and loveable, but can only accept rats in anthropomorphised form. Rats even took the rap for the millions who died in the Black Death when it was actually fleas what did it.

Not Ratty, but Ratsputin.

The Mad Russian Monk ate poisoned cakes with relish and had to be shot and drowned before he succumbed. Ratty is obviously equally immune. What's more, he looked bright-eyed and, if not bushy-tailed, sleek and fit when he arrived at the feeding box this morning.

My wife says he looks bigger and fitter because it is not Ratty, but perhaps a relative. He too must be given the Mars bar treatment.

I said I would see to it, but I like to think our visitor is indeed Ratty, and that makes me feel less of a killer. I did cut up another Mars bar and put the chunks into the box this afternoon, but forgot to add the poison.

~

Nearly a month before we start shooting, but for we actors there's much to do in preparation.

This morning was my first visit to the location unit HQ at Newport for a check on my measurements for Sergeant Westfield's uniform. While there I had the first of what will be weekly tests to prove I positively have not got the Covid 19 infection.

In spite of the warm weather, I wore my Russian Cossack hat and long leather overcoat. It is actually not that long, but the original owner must have had much longer legs than me. When my wife asked why I was dressed up like that, I said I wanted to look like an actor. She sniffed and said I looked more like a homeless man in midwinter.

At the site and in spite of my age, I felt a melange of nerves, anticipation and excitement as we arrived in a car park awash with a jumble of fake police cars, portable toilets, dining cars, snaking lines of cable and huge spotlights on gantries.

While Donella waited in the car, and, I noticed, slid down in the seat, I picked my way through the paraphernalia of film production as if it was an every day experience. At the entrance I adjusted my dress, swept through the glass doors and made a booming announcement that Sergeant Westcliff had arrived.

The girl at the reception desk looked unimpressed and pointed with her pen to her left. 'We do surgical appliances,' she said: 'Acting is next door.'

~

'Can you please stop shouting like Brian Blessed on speed? And I'm not going in there till you take that silly hat and coat off."

We have come to Godshill to celebrate with tea and cake my first encounter with the production department.

After a swab test to prove I was free of Covid 19, I was ushered into a room filled with young women sitting at computers and sewing machines. Amongst serried racks of costumes I had been measured up for my uniform, hat and even a pair of regulation police service shoes. When I asked for advice about shaving my beard off or dying my hair to look more the part, the lady with the tape measure raised an eyebrow and said I would have to take that up with Make-Up. To me, she said, I looked just fine. As I returned to the car with a spring in my step, I realised why my great age for a working policeman may have gone unremarked. To young people, everyone over fifty looks equally ancient which would include some policemen and any really old people playing them.

Around a couple of million visitors arrive on the Isle of Wight every year and leave a half a billion pounds behind. It's not known exactly how many of them visit the village of Godshill, but I bet it's a lot.

Although the strip of Olde Worlde Tea Shoppes, cider brewers and craft outlets look like a modern fabrication of film set, Godshill pre-dates the Domesday Book and the 14th-century church sits above a site of pagan worship. Legend has it that building began at the bottom of the hill, but each morning the masons would arrive to find the heavy stones had been moved to the top. After this had happened a few times, the builders got the message that God would prefer his house at the top of the hill, which is what happened and, of course, where the name of the village comes from.

The huddle of thatched cottages around and below the church were built for labourers and masons on the job, but now form the core to what has become the most visited village on the Island.

For more energetic visitors, there's also bags to see and enjoy all around the village. You can walk for miles along well-signed bridleways and footpaths, through woods and alongside streams and across meadows and through farmyards and all for free.

The last time here I took the footpath alongside the Tudor-chimneyed Griffin and followed what must be one of the longest continual uphill treks on the Island. As with the village, the skein of pathways are very well groomed and maintained, and the views are spectacular.

At the top I stood and looked around the great bowl of green and the doll's house roofs of Wroxall far below, then started the climb down to a place of drama, tragedy and intrigue.

Once the grandest home on the Island, Appuldurcombe House is a fine example of early

18th century Baroque architecture and was the seat of the Worsley family.

All went fairly smoothly for the owners until Sir Richard Worsley inherited the property in 1768 and met and married a wealthy heiress and wild child Seymour Fleming. It was recorded that he married her '…for love and £80,000.'

While he was busy defending the Island from attacks by France, Spain and Holland, his good lady was working her way through the top roués and blades of the time. It is said she was the inspiration for the notorious Lady Teazle in Sheridan's *School for Scandal*. When the cuckolded husband took exception to one of her lovers, a notorious court case revealed that he was number twenty-eight on her hit list.

Scandal followed and when Sir Richard died of

apoplexy, Appuldurcombe passed through the hands of a variety of relatives. It left the family hands in 1855 and was launched as a grand hotel. This venture failed and it became an academy for young gentlemen. At the turn of the century Appuldurcombe became home for the hundred Benedictine monks who would later take over at Quarr Abbey. Troops were billeted in the grand but fading and increasingly dishevelled house during both World Wars, and what was to be the final blow came in 1943. A Luftwaffe Dornier delivered a mine close to the building before crashing nearby, and the bomb caused significant damage.

From a distance, you can imagine just how grand Appuldurcombe was, and the great bowl in which it sits makes the perfect setting. The landscaped grounds particularly took my fancy, and that was before I learned that much of the work had been carried out under the supervision of Capability Brown.

Nowadays, Appuldurcombe is in the capable hands of English Heritage and is said to be one of the most haunted places on the Isle of Wight, which, given the Island's spook count, is certainly saying something.

~

We are paying for our cream tea with a hike up to another distinctive Island landmark.

Looking like a medieval imagining of what a rocket ship might look like in some far-distant future, the tower of St Catherine's Oratory* stands at the top of a steep-ish climb.

The tower is all that remains of what was built in 1328 by a local landowner. In those days, rich and powerful people could literally get away with murder by lobbing a significant sum into a project approved of by the Church. Sometimes the goodwill payment would go straight into the pocket of an influential member of the clergy. In this case, the building of the oratory was the penance for local landowner, whose offence had been the looting of a wrecked ship laden with casks of white wine on their way to a monastery in Picardy.

His way to escape threatened excommunication and eternal damnation in the fires took the form of a lighthouse with an oratory attached. As well as paying for the building, the penitent was required to make an endowment which would maintain a priest to look after the lighthouse and say masses for those lost at sea.

Because of the lighthouse appendage, the oratory stands at one of the highest points on the Island. It is a delightful place to be and look out over the land and sea and think of when the great blocks of stone were hauled up the slope and work began. That alone makes it well worth the climb.

*From the Latin oratorium an oratory was a place of prayer, or the art of eloquence.

~

Close to the Oratory downs is what is officially the oldest theme park in the UK, and some say the whole wide world.

Blackgang Chine dates back to the first half of the 19th century, when an enterprising Victorian took out a lease for an amusement park which would incorporate the spectacular ravine. Customers flocked to climb up and down the stairway and marvel at the floral displays.

Nowadays there are animatronic dinosaurs Strutting their stuff, and I think even kids who are veterans of the likes of Thorpe Park would be impressed. Especially when they learn that they are walking where real dinosaurs once roamed and that Steven Spielberg considered this place as the setting for Jurassic Park. Another more tenuous link is that Walt Disney's uncle lived not far away from the new attraction. It is just possible that he could have passed the idea on to his nephew, Walt and sowed the seeds of what was to come in the shape of Disneylands and Worlds. Far-fetched perhaps, but stranger things have happened on the Isle of Wight.

~

Good news for us, and bad news for ever-rapacious property developers.

Freshwater has won the battle to be awarded the site of the new primary school and the millions to build it. With surprising firmness, the council say this is a final decision and there will be no further debate.

Yarmouth has not been altogether gracious, but to us it seems completely logical that a new primary school should be built in the place where nearly all its pupils live.

The work is due to start next year, Covid-19 allowing.

I passed the other day and saw that someone had already taped over the name of the old school on the gate. It will be sad to see the old building disappear and there will obviously be some noise from the site. Somehow, I think the sound of a new school being built will be much less of an annoyance than the appearance of yet another pug-ugly estate of irritatingly uniform houses that nobody wants except those who throw them up.

~

It is not only the house and garage that are on the move.

It's less than a month before filming and potential disaster has struck.

I was cleaning my teeth with my new turbo-drive brush on full throttle this morning when I felt something in my mouth give.

It was a nerve-jangling sensation, and exploring, I found that one of my front teeth had suddenly become loose.

This could be very bad news. It's impossible to sign up with a local dentist, and my future as an actor could be in the balance. I don't know what it says in the contract about teeth, but I can't see the director being too pleased if I turn up looking like Nobby Styles after the 1966 World Cup soccer triumph.

∞∞∞∞

14

"During the last invasion of this country, hundreds of French troops landed on the foreshore nearby. This armed invasion was bloodily defeated and repulsed by local Militia. 21st July 1545"

The inscription on a plaque at Seaview, a village on the north-eastern coast. The account has been disputed as an exaggeration, but it is true that the Island was a frequent destination for French visitors on an awayday trip.

The most Indian of summers lingers, but winter waits in the wings.

It is my favourite time of year, but then, so are all the times of year when in the countryside. Living in a town, you just turn the heating on or open a window to accommodate the change of seasons. In the countryside you get the full flavour.

West Wight is not exactly France *profonde*, but I have to admit that the longer I'm here, the more I feel at home. Familiarity with this fascinating Island is far from breeding contempt, and I feel not the slightest itchiness in either foot.

I think the Island is growing on me because in so many ways it seems more like living in a foreign land than a part of the Kingdom.

I think another reason I grow so fond and thus protective of our new home is the way so many people on the mainland look down their noses at us. It's true that some things are done differently here, but that just makes us different, not lesser. From what I have seen, Wighteans quite like having a low crime rate and plenty of room to breathe and time to take their time. Those who don't like that situation and attitude don't have to live or even come here, of course.

~

One thing's for sure, and that is that the Isle of Wight is a very good place to be while a world-wide pandemic is raging. The UK has the worst figures for deaths in Europe, but I think other countries will catch up before it is all over.

Another irrelevant but important benefit to us moving here, as my wife points out, is that had we stayed in Brittany, I would probably not be embarking on a late flowering career as an actor.

That's true, but unless I sort the wobbly tooth situation the flower might die before its full bloom.

~

As we settle in, so hopefully does our new home. The Crack of Doom has not re-appeared in my office, and we have got used to the bathroom door opening of its own accord. I wouldn't like to risk opening all three garage doors at the same time, but it is still standing.

~

My wife often chides me for accosting total strangers while out walking. What she does not know is that I am very careful about who I pick on.

Certainly not nervous- looking women, and care needs to be taken with either gender who sport tattoos, any sort of face jewellery and a fierce-looking dog. I also avoid people who want to share too much of themselves and their past and present lives. My wife says I should also steer clear of people who look like me, though I don't know what she means by that.

This morning I was labouring up Golden Hill and overtook an elderly man and his dog. The dog was on the lead and despite its size looked as if he was helping pull his master up the slope. I made some throwaway remark about him being the first person

I had overtaken in years and we both stopped to get our breaths and compare medical notes. This is what older people do.

My partner in breathlessness said he was over eighty, and showed me a gadget slung round his neck which would alert his wife if he did not come back from the daily walk.

When I asked if he was a caulkhead, he said yes, and that before retirement he had run the tobacconists in the village. Before that he had served with the Metropolitan police, and then in Bermuda. He quite casually mentioned that he had been on duty when the Governor and his aide were assassinated by the Black Panther movement in the 70s, and that he had had some 'dealings' with them. He would not say more, and we parted at the car park. I watched him make his slow and painful way to the car and thought about how hard it can be to see beyond the years and now and what people might have been and done. And what stories they have to tell if you ask them.

Today we're heading for the far East.

Ironically, one of the most appealing aspects of the Island for us is what puts a lot of people off the idea of living here. They think they'd feel trapped and become bored with the same surroundings. What they don't get is just how diverse the Isle of Wight is, and how places change with the seasons, weather and even mood. It's almost as if the strictures of the sea magnify and concentrate the differences between the areas and the towns and villages in them.

We are only an hour from the easternmost point, but in between there are hills and dales and beaches and cliffs and forests galore. There are also busy towns and tucked-away hamlets and villages and in-your-face resorts to suit your needs and mood. And all with their very own distinct character.

A very good example of a place being of but unlike the rest of the Island lies in an area which is as close as you can get to France without falling into the sea.

Niton sits almost at the southern tip of the rough diamond, and is well-stocked for pubs and churches and a post office where you can buy a paper and take a cup of tea or a stronger drink while you do your business there. Sitting and watching young mums taking the kids to school and elderly ladies on their way with stick and shopping bag to the village shop shows you what a real community looks like.

Not because people are that different from the mainland, just less in number. That means everyone knows everyone else and their business. This might not sound very appealing, but it certainly keeps the crime rate down. There are not too many tattoos on show at Niton, but neither any evidence of graffiti or vandalism or high or low-level misdeeds.

Just down the road from the village proper is the oldest still-standing lighthouse on the Island. Work started at St Catherine's Point in 1840 in response to a shipwreck off Blackgang Chine. The Clarendon was returning from the West Indies with an 'exotic' cargo of coconuts and rum, and twenty-three souls were lost in the gale-force winds. All but one were washed ashore, the exception being a Miss Gourlay. Hard to believe, but it is recorded that her body was taken by the tide or some supernatural intervention across the Solent to come to rest at the foot of her father's garden in Southsea.

Cows were said to have stampeded in fear when the great light was first lit, and St Catherine's was one of the few lighthouses in the world to be powered by electricity. In 1888 the state-of-the-art arc lamps could be seen an incredible eighteen miles out to sea.

Just along the coast, from Ventnor and close to Niton, St Lawrence is a pretty exclusive and expensive place. This is in spite of - or even because of - a collapse that caused the closure of the coastal road and effectively cut the village off from the rest of the Island. The residents can get out, but nobody can drive past their homes on the once-busy but now eerily quiet road.

Added to the appeal is the interesting and some-times slightly risky walks along the cliff and up and down strangely conical mounds with corkscrew pathways. Then there's the corking 16-th century pub called the Buddle Inn to hand, as characterful and atmospheric as can be.

Overall and as is so common on the Island, this fascinating corner is very much of itself as well as part of a whole.

Long-standing: Niton Lighthouse

It's a curious sensation to be on solid ground and yet look down from above on aeroplanes as they land and take off.

We're sitting outside the really pubby pub atop Culver Cliff or, as some prefer to call it, Culver Down. Just a mile or so along the coast, it's a wild and rugged place and as different from Sandown as you could imagine.

The lofty promontory is famed internationally as the home of a particularly rare sort of ant, and sadly known locally as a chosen spot for ending one's life by driving rather than jumping over the edge into eternity. Near to the pub is a row of former coastguard cottages with what must be some of the finest views on the Island.

~

For some reason, the airfield at Sandown puts me in mind of Biggin Hill as seen in the *Battle of Britain* movie. And by that, I mean before the Luftwaffe bombing and strafing raids scene.

Planes are taking off and landing constantly, and surprisingly for the busiest airfield in the land, Sandown is staffed mainly by volunteers. This, I hope, does not include those in charge of the Control Tower.

Technically, the airfield is what is known as an unlicensed aerodrome, though I'm sure that is not the same sort of thing as running an unlicensed bar or betting shop. There are no direct flights from elsewhere on the mainland, but a regular service from Southampton.

Many years ago, my wife and I went on a flight from here around the Island in a near-vintage plane which looked well past its Best Fly Before date. It was owned and flown and I suspect maintained by a couple of cheery old-ish gents, wearing what looked like pucka WWII leather flying helmets. Disappointingly, neither sported a Flying Officer Kite moustache, but both looked truly at home in the cockpit and of an age that made me wonder if they had seen action in WWII. They certainly displayed the casual attitude adopted by the RAF heroes in those dark and dangerous years, and our pilot spent quite a lot of time turning round and placing an elbow on the back of his seat so he could have a friendly chat with the passengers. It was a little unnerving to see him let go of the wheel, but his partner would reach over and give it a tweak if necessary.

Times change even on the Isle of Wight, and I read that the modern version of a must-try pleasure flight around the Island is a ride in one of the Spitfire replicas that drone over Golden Hill every afternoon. They set off from an airport on the mainland, and offer a variety of pricing options. I read that the 'entry level' flight is a snip at £2,750 and will 'deliver' you a full thirty minutes in the air. If you really want to splash out, you and a friend can go for the 45-minute Fighter Appreciation Experience at just £12,000. I note that all flights allow you to touch the controls and sort-of fly the plane yourself.

The glowing article in the local paper reminded me of my first flight around the Island. We were leaving a boozy wedding reception in Chichester when a friend asked if we fancied a buzz around the Island in his little Auster, which was conveniently parked at Goodwood. Totally irresponsibly we said of course and I climbed into the back while my wife sat next to the driver.

The several pints of black velvet kicked in, and I fell asleep soon after take-off. I woke and it was a curious sensation to find myself on a level with and in eye contact with a bemused motorist keeping pace with us along the cliff road approaching the Needles. I waved and he waved, then I sat up and saw that my wife was flying the plane. Our friend was lighting a cigarette and making encouraging sounds, but I made sure he took over before we reached and flew around rather than into the jagged white fingers of rock.

~

The road alongside Sandown airfield passes close to what looks like an interesting bar. I think it might be the original club house, bought and tinkered with thirty years ago by a friend who thought he was a reincarnation of the Bloody Red Baron.

Oscar Ebenezer Brown was a little, round man who ran a scrap-yard in Sussex after leaving London's East End, as he told us, at the invitation of Ronnie and Reggie Kray.

Nowadays, lots of people work hard to portray eccentric 'characters' and tell us what loonies they are for jumping off high places on the end of an elastic band or playing the ukulele upside down. Oscar Brown was a real, proper character. He lived in a sprawling and decrepit manor house in Hampshire he had bought for almost a song when it was due to be pulled down to make way for a motorway. As it happened it was not and we always wondered if he had some sort of prior knowledge.

Oscar spent his day knocking down walls and making vast vats of Irish stew for family and friends. When he had made the main house uninhabitable, he moved his unfortunate wife and sons into the lodge and carried on with what he called the improvement works. When not attacking the building, he would be playing with the parts of his1953 Dino Ferrari. He had taken the very, very valuable sports car to bits and forgotten which bit went where.

He also quite genuinely believed himself to be the reincarnation of Manfred Von Richtoven the notorious World War I air ace. Oscar was a keen flier and liked to emulate some of the Red Baron's stunts, and we last saw him when he bought the old clubhouse at Sandown and moved in. The plan was to turn it into a bar for like-minded enthusiasts so they could have a drink and some Irish stew before taking off to loop-the-loop. Being Oscar, he took the building to bits but never got round to putting it back together again before he died. We still miss him and think of him often, and also of how they really don't make them like that anymore.

~

We are currently passing through serious caravan park territory.

Whitecliff Bay Holiday Park advertises itself as a hidden gem, and it is true that it is well away from the road and with some wondrous free views and a sweeping, sheltered beach. It is a good, honest and safe place for families with young children and on-line praise is hearty. I like caravan holidays as they remind you of how comfortable you are at home.

We're in a place where some homes and their views are reckoned beyond the price of rubies. At the opposite end of the Island, it's almost its mirror-image in terms of poshness and property prices.

It is another Island idiosyncrasy how very up-market and very much *not* upmarket places can rub shoulders. With no disrespect to our home village, Yarmouth and Freshwater are a fair example.

Ryde and Bembridge are a handful of miles apart and share the same coastline and sea water, but could not be further apart in property values and perhaps esteem.

Bembridge began life as five small hamlets, and by the Middle Ages had developed its main activities of fishing, exporting the very desirable local limestone and importing smuggled goods. Then in 1545, the village was invaded and fired by a French fleet. It was a ruse to tempt the English fleet to leave the safety of Portsmouth harbour, but the plan didn't work. The provocation did, however, result in Henry VIII's pride and joy flagship Mary Rose setting out and immediately sinking in the Solent as the king watched aghast from Southsea Castle. Not a shot had been fired in anger, and the tragedy was put down to having too many noble onlookers and too few skilled crew on board. I was running Portsmouth's local radio station when the wreck was being recovered in the late 1970s, and put the soundtrack together for the Mary Rose exhibition at the Naval Base. Millions of people must have heard the audio representation of the great ship sinking with all hands, and few would guess it was actually the sound of a volcano exploding being played backwards.

~

We pass the houseboat village and pause to pay homage at the famed Crab & Lobster Inn. It has long specialised in living up to its name and serving up fruits of the sea. The pub has a great reputation though we have not eaten there. That's not because

All that remains of the 12th century church at St Helens. Sailors would take stones to scrub the decks, from where the universal Royal Naval term 'holystoning' came.

we think the food is overpriced, just that we are too mean to pay the price of eating good food from someone else's table.

On through St Helens, a pleasant village of a thousand souls, living round what are said to be one of the largest village greens in the land.

Next, to Nettlestone to drop into the Isle of Wight Distillery to check out the Mermaid Pink Gin before a cup of tea at Puckpool, once a sumptuous Swiss Cottage and then a defence battery and now a holiday park.

Our day ends at Seaview. The sandy Priory Bay can only be reached at low tide, and has an interesting outlook to Palmerstonian forts and the mainland beyond.

The locally named Millionaire's Row is nearby and when I was editor of *Food & Drink* magazine I ate a scarily expensive (had I been settling the bill) but wonderful meal in a swish restaurant which had once been a bank. It had in fact once been voted the Prettiest Bank in Britain. Nowadays I would guess it takes in more deposits a day than it ever did as a branch of Lloyds.

This is certainly an interestingly diverse part of the Island and has attracted some interestingly diverse people. Amongst them were Margaret Thatcher, who liked to holiday at Seaview, and film star David Niven, who spent his early years in Bembridge. Spending his final years in the village was Jet Harris, former bass guitar player with Cliff Richard and The Shadows and performer of the 60s smash hit classics *Diamonds* and *Scarlett O'Hara*.

It has been an interesting day and one that has

reflected the richness and diversity of land and seascapes, as well as the communities that dwell within them.

15

"All this beauty is of God"

The Isle of Wight motto.

We woke this morning just twenty-odd miles from our home, but it was like being on holiday in another part of the country.

As I've been banging on about repeatedly, it seems a peculiarly Isle of Wightean property that different parts of the rough diamond are very, well, different. That might not seem to make much sense, but people who live or like coming here will know what I mean. It may be because we are surrounded by the sea, which magnifies the differences within our small county. Or even that the locals choose to magnify them. Whatever the reason, it is true. For sure I would not feel that difference if I drove from Portsmouth to Southampton. Indeed, those two grimy and overstuffed cities would seem depressingly samey to most visitors.

Another effect of waking up to a different view from the window is that it has made my feet begin to itch. Given what an endlessly interesting and diverse the Island is proving, though, it's much less of an itch than when we arrived.

~

It's clearly not only me who thinks the Island a very different place. A lot of people seem to think it's a foreign country.

Doing some on-line research over breakfast, I find that Frequently Asked Questions include:

What is the Isle of Wight made of?
What is the currency?
Is it okay to bring pets?
What language do they speak?
Are there any supermarkets?
Are there any nightclubs?
What side of the road do they drive on?

~

Brading is one of the oldest towns on the Island,

and dates back to the time of Alfred the Great. It sits on the western bank of the other river Yar and is surrounded by an area rightly adjudged to be of Outstanding Natural Beauty. There are the remains of a Roman Villa, a thriving vineyard/winery, and once upon a time the village was a port, with ships heaving to outside the Bugle in the High Street.

In my childhood, no visit to the area was complete without venturing into the Waxwork Museum. We are much more hardened nowadays, but in its heyday, The Chamber of Horrors was said to give visitors recurring nightmares. Other features to marvel at included a breathing, foot-tapping wax-work of Queen Victoria, a stuffed elephant, a flying cat and an organ-playing skeleton. Tastes and time change, and, sadly to me, the museum has gone the way of so many entertainments which gave such pleasure in simpler times.

Surrounded as it is by the haunting, silent beauty of the marshes, it seems to us that the constant groan, whine and roar of through-traffic stands out in harsh contrast. There are degrees of traffic in-your-facedness, and I would put Brading at about an eight out of ten. Fine for people who don't mind noise or are profoundly deaf, but not those of a more sensitive disposition.

When looking for a new home, we visited a three-storey town house which seemed almost suspiciously cheap for what it was. The terraced villa was laid out and finished beautifully, with scrubbed wooden floors, high ceilings, winding staircases and whitewashed walls, with outside a real deal-clincher. The back garden featured a cantilevered platform with table and chairs, looking out over the river to the serene and beautiful marshlands beyond.

After leaving and standing on the pavement and watching and hearing the torrent of cars and lorries and coaches whizzing by just yards away, we knew the lovely house was not for us. As my wife said, people who live on noisy roads must get used to it, or perhaps not be bothered by it. Within months of moving in, she forecast, I would develop a tic, begin to foam at the mouth and spend my time standing on the pavement pointing a hair dryer at the passing vehicles as if it were a speed gun.

I know I keep on about the problem of through-traffic in some otherwise idyllic villages, but just ask the people who live there what they think. Of course, we are as much part of the problem as any other driver and I don't know the solution. You cannot by-pass every enchanting town or village, and it can only get worse before it gets better. If it ever does.

Next on our dawdle home through what is known as the 'bowl' of the Island was a visit to the ancient woodland of Borthwood Copse. It was a delight to leave the car and walk up to the viewpoint at Kite Hill to admire the only surviving windmill on the Island and look for dormice and red squirrels. Although they are said to gather in great numbers here, we saw neither. Even so it is a most pleasant place to spend some quality time in the bosom of nature.

~

The Bembridge Windmill

This is a particularly enterprising part of the Island, awash with creative commercial concerns like the Isle of Wight Shipwreck Centre, Robin Hill Adventure Park, a cheese farm, Havenstreet Steam Railway and even a Brass Rubbing Centre.

Nowadays, the Fighting Cocks is an impeccably family-friendly pub, but gets its name from what went on down the road at Wackland. Here, the ever-boisterous squire William Thatcher was renowned as a breeder of countless, bloody-spurred killers.

In my reporting days, I spent a day in this part of the Island and particularly at a pub owned by a former oompah-playing member of the Temperance Seven band, and a stately home owned by a freshly-ennobled businessman from Birmingham.

He followed a long line of distinguished occupants, including Alfred the Great, William the Conqueror and Henry VIII.

When I arrived with tape recorder and notebook at Arreton Manor in 1977, I found Count Pomeroy du Slade an unassuming chap with a Brummie accent. As he told me, he had changed his name by deed poll from plain Mr Slade to more suit his new surroundings. His wife was a charming lady who sat in the entrance hall and took the punters money.

The Count and his Lady are long gone, and the place is up for sale. For the history alone it's a huge bargain at a couple of million quid. It is not known if our current monarch is interested in adding to the royal pedigree, but I intend buying it as soon as my ship of dreams, best-ever best-seller or Lotto jackpot win comes in.

~

We are on the way home from our foreign break and a visit to the garlic farm at Newchurch. It is very successful, which is strange when you think that a couple of generations ago you wouldn't have been able to give the odiferous bulbs away. Nowadays, people queue up pay to walk around the farm, visit the restaurant and buy varieties of the onion or take home a jar of garlic pickle, mayo or even jam.

This has given me an idea as a fall-back if book sales dry up and my new acting career does not take off. My idea for a virtual dog website never materialised after an informal survey of likely interest, but our visit to the garlic farm has sparked off a new idea. If people will flock to the garlic farm, why would they not beat a trail to one that breeds snails? Like garlic, people who would have been horrified at the idea of eating a mollusc now pay a small fortune to hook them out of their shells in a posh restaurant. It would surely be a very low start-up investment to rent a field and stock it with snails. Of course, they would need to be proper edible type and imported from across the Channel, but after that it would be nearly all pure profit. We could charge people to come and watch our free-range snails gambolling in the open pastures, and they could take a box-full away still alive or artfully presented in-shell. I also reckon if we did a deal with the garlic farm and fed our stock with their butter, they could be sold ready-flavoured.

~

My daily stroll to the village paper shop. It's a comforting routine, and I like being a regular at the newsagent, confectioners, fancy goods and art supplies shop run by Edward G Robinson and family.

In fact, as his hair and beard grow untrammelled from beneath his beret, Francis the owner looks more how Che Guevara might have appeared had he survived into old age. Francis relies heavily on his walking stick nowadays, but as he says, his mind is still in good health. He is an interesting man, starting life on the Orkney Isles and deciding to finish it on an island at the other end of the kingdom. Today he told me he is a Freeman of the City of London, meaning he could drive a flock of sheep over London Bridge if he were so minded. We talk for a while about art and Life and then I pick up a copy of the local paper and dally to chat with Matthew, son of Francis. Matthew is of middle age and a truly gentle man, and we often pass on the tracks above the village as he pedals around on newspaper delivery duty.

Reflecting on the satisfactory slow pace of village life and the pleasure of conversation, I leave the shop and step off the pavement. All at once the banshee shriek of a speeding two-stroke motorbike at top revs and low gear splits the air and I retreat to safety. The rider must be doing almost twice the speed limit, and the noise is more than aggressive. People wince and actually recoil as the machine speeds up the slope and disappears. He may have gone but the sound continues.

I cross the road and reach the sports centre when the noise and its cause returns. People scatter as the rider skids twice around the parking area and then makes for the exit and me. I think about it, then stand my ground. He screeches to a stop, jockeying the throttle and looking at me with narrowed eyes through the gap between helmet and the scarf around his face. We maintain the tableau for what seems a long moment, then he makes as if to get off the bike. I try to look bigger and younger and fiercer, and luckily for me he doesn't dismount. He probably thinks I am not worth the trouble.

After another glare, he shakes his head as if in bemusement at the behaviour of this old fool, lets the clutch lever in and screams around me. I give a small sigh of relief, shoulder my staff and continue my walk and think about the man and why he is like he is and does what he does. For certain, his behaviour must diminish the quality of life for thousands of people within earshot every day. Perhaps he doesn't care, or actually wants to do just that. It's no good telling me I am old and grumpy and he may be a good man who is kind to his elderly mother and dumb animals and does charity work. I would bet my house he isn't, and doesn't. He probably just thinks that indulging his idea of fun trumps everyone else's rights not to alarmed, irritated or scared. They say nowadays that noise pollution is as damaging to our health as any other type. If those who enforce our rules attended to small matters like this rather than turning a deaf ear, life would surely be better in a small but important way.

~

Back to proper village life.

Turning on to the track up to the allotments, I see it's dropping-off time at the primary school.

Having walked rather than driven their children here, the mums are gathered at the entrance and seem loath to leave. Apart from the clothes and hair styles, modern buggies and the odd tattoo, the scene is little different from when I went to a school just like this one. The remarkable thing is that rather than standing together while talking to someone else on a mobile phone, the mums are actually talking to each other. Another difference from the norm in these sad times is that nobody looks at me suspiciously as I walk by. Indeed, most respond to my greeting with a smile.

A little further up the track I see a couple staring up into the branches of a poplar tree. I see that the man is taking lots of pictures with a proper camera, while the woman excitedly points at whatever it is he is snapping.

As I arrive, the man shows me a series of images on the panel on the back of his camera, and explains it is a red squirrel. Thinking they are visitors, I show interest and say there are several thousand living on the Island. A little huffily, he says that may be so, but this is the first one he and his wife have seen since they moved here three years ago.

I congratulate them and go on my way, wondering if their squirrel was our squirrel, or if there might be all of two living in and amongst the hundreds of acres of woodland round our home.

~

I am to be found in the allotment greenhouse, giving my aubergines a pep talk.

On the seed packet they are a deeply lustrous and plumptious purple-black and as shiny as if they have been coated with yacht varnish. On the vine, mine look wan, weary and on the point of expiry. I don't know if talking to them will help, but if it works for HRH Prince Charles, I can't see what harm it can do for me to try. Indeed, recent claims indicate they may understand the tenor if not words of a good talking to.

Just to make us feel even worse about what we get up to on the planet, some scientists are now alleging that plants are sentient, and in essence are living, feeling beings. Bad enough to be censored for enjoying a pork chop, but now vegetables will be off the menu for those who choose to listen to the nutty professors.

To however small a degree, the damage is done. The next time I am peeling freshly cooked beetroot and the red tined water spirals down the sink I know it will put me in mind of the shower scene in Psycho and make me wonder if I have committed murder most foul.

Giving up on the aubergines, I look through the local paper and read about a man who has made a working model aeroplane from plastic drinks bottles.

The lead story is about a dog found wandering around on Ventnor beach, confused and disoriented. His condition was because he had found and eaten a pile of human faeces containing strong traces of cannabis resin. The owner told the reporter that Bentley the golden retriever had spent two days under the effect of the drug, and that it was a growing problem when people ate chocolate or other foods laced with marijuana, then defecated on the beach.

Putting the paper aside, I take down and re-read

the postcard stuck into the frame above the workbench. It shows the bridge at Avignon, and came with news from Will.

Like doctors and other professionals, his writing is barely legible, but I can make out that he is in his favourite part of France. He has been sleeping in the *foyers* first set up as billets for soldiers in World War One, and now acting as overnight hostels for people passing through and allegedly seeking work. So far he has resisted the temptation to, as he puts it, bilk a hotel, but he is fed up with sleeping in the same room as men with even smellier feet than his own.

He also reports that he has paid homage at the White House in Arles where his long-time hero Vincent Van Gogh lived briefly with Paul Gaugin, and had a glass of the weaker modern version of *absinthe* in a nearby café where the couple are said to have indulged in the Green Fairy.

Will concludes by hoping we are well and thanking us again for our hospitality, but adds that he will not be returning to the Isle of Wight next summer. It is a beautiful place, he says, but his heart lies in France and time flies faster as the years go by. Soon, he knows, he will end up drooling in a chair with his mind gone, and he must make the most of what he has left in the place where he wants most to be.

I think about our times with the White Horses of the Camargue and watching a pink cloud of flamingos rising from the marshes, and nod in accord. Proust may be long, but life is short, and we must all make the most of what we are given.

The post brings more reams of information about locations, work days and scripts for all the scenes in which I will not appear.

There's also notice of an appointment with a doctor in Ryde for a comprehensive medical check-up. It is for insurance purposes, my agent assures me in a note; every actor in the production has to have one and they are not picking me out because of my age and any chance that I might peg out before shooting finishes.

Apart from the fear that I will not be able to learn my lines or will make a mess of my walk-on scenes, I'm getting quite excited as the time for my appearances approaches.

Filming is already taking place all over the Island and particularly in West Wight. Taped to signposts in remote locations are day-glow posters bearing arrows and cryptic messages like 'TBMD shoot for Sc. V. starters'. The other day I walked to the bay

and found a long string of giant fairy lights hanging on bushes and leading to a marquee with a catering van under siege alongside. I deliberately crossed the road and walked down a lane to where a film crew were holding a camera and lights just inches from the face of a woman sitting in a car. A large young man with a clipboard saw me coming and stepped forward, but I forestalled him by holding a hand up in a 'I-know-how-it-works' gesture and whispering 'It's okay, I'm Sergeant Westfield.' I don't think he knew what I meant, but he nervously directed me to a pathway to one side of the action.

In my rucksack is the book on which the series is very loosely based, and I've been reading it during my afternoon yomps across the downs. There is no mention of Sergeant Westfield so far, but then the book seems to bear little relation to the scripts I have seen.

The Beast Must Die was written under a pen name in 1938 by one of our most eminent Poet Laureates, Cecil Day-Lewis. It was one of a successful series featuring gentleman private investigator Nigel Strangeways. It is very much of its time, and the TV adaptation has changed characters and genders and locations. But it could change our lives.

I'm still undecided about the part pre-determination plays in our lives, but it does seem curious that someone decided to set the series in the place where I have just arrived, and, even curiouser, has picked me to play one of the characters. Perhaps it is Fate opening the door to a very late career opportunity. As long, that is, as I can remember to get my lines right and not walk into any furniture.

~

A chirpy weatherman is advising listeners to 'eye the sky' as I get ready to tread the Strangeways serpent's tail.

He says that if the sky is blue, it's good news. If there are dark clouds and it is overcast, that is not so good and we should all take care to wrap up and wear 'appropriate' clothing. I sit down and think about phoning in to ask which boot to put on which foot, and ask if he thinks I will get wet if it rains.

~

Few villages can claim their own forests, but Brighstone is one. It is the largest stretch of concentrated woodland on the Island and sits atop the spine alongside the Tennyson Trail from Freshwater to Carisbrooke Castle, which is my destination today. It can be light and airy or dark and mysterious dependent on time of day and year and awash with walks and life and atmosphere. It's open to riders and cyclists as well as walkers but is a fair climb from the nearest car park. This is good for me and because there are so many woodland rides and trails it is rare to have a human encounter. Van Gogh said if you love nature, you can see beauty everywhere, and I like to admire it on my own.

~

If this were a formal travel guide, I would probably write that the village of Brighstone nestles between the downs and the coast, which to be fair it does.

For me, it's another beautifully balanced, living (rather than dormitory) Island village. Together with an ancient water mill and other photogenic reminders of the past, there's a doctor's surgery, a post office, community library, thatched newspaper shop and an excellent pub. Best of all, ancient meets modern with a terrific village store. Fruit and veg, firelighters, kindling, bags of charcoal and fresh flowers are displayed outside on tiers of planks and crates in the proper, traditional way. Inside are to be found home-baked bread and fancies, and certainly the best Hampshire lardy cake we can find on the Island.

The only disturbance to the smooth passage of village life is the evidence of new bricks and mortar sprouting on green fields close by the ancient church. This disturbs those who like things the way they are. Like many who live in peaceful villages on the Island, they feel and fear the sound of cement mixers at their backs.

It is a stealthy advance and the newbuilds come in platoons rather than battalions, but they keep coming.

Somehow this continual bolting-on of a handful of new homes for the wealthy can seem worse than creating a modern village somewhere inoffensive.

Ironically, an article in the local paper last week reported that the Isle of Wight has one of the worst records in Britain for achieving its target for house-building. The target for the past three years was nearly two thousand, but less than a thousand appeared. The Island Council is said to be concerned that this shortfall will lead to pressure on them to allow building in unsuitable areas to make up the shortfall.

There may be no direct correlation, but the constant cry to build more and more new housing stock seems at odds on an Island where one in ten homes stand empty. The character of villages is developed over many years, and I hope that the people who dole out planning permission have thought it through. If they get it wrong, it will be too late to start again.

~

Following the serpent's tail, I pass the well-thatched hamlet of Limerstone and the Mary Case farm, known for its traditional variety of English apples, honey and farmer's markets.

Next is the Shorwell chute. leading down to the pretty village with a thatched store where a duck is said to be a frequent caller. Nearby there's an attractive old pub, a variety of woodland and downland walks, and overall a certain Dibley-esque air. I didn't check it out, but I do hope the village also sports a suitably Junoesque lady vicar and a mostly certifiable parish council.

~

Unsurprisingly and not counting a redundant chalk quarry and a stunning view, the first thing to catch your eye at Chillerton Down is the transmitting station. It soars to a majestic height of nearly two hundred and twenty-nine metres, and it's very stolid modernity and steeliness makes for me an attractive contrast to the surrounding soft timelessness of vale and dale.

Chillerton originally transmitted signals for Southern Television, but now handles a number of local and mainland radio stations. All around is another walker's paradise, and there's a nine-mile yomping challenge starting and finishing at the Chequers

Inn at Rookley. I don't know if you get a pint for completing it, but it has set me thinking about what would make an exciting challenge involving the transmitter. As I sit on one of the huge concrete anchoring blocks, it occurred to me how cool it would be to hold what they call an edificeering or skywalking yearly competition here. The Chillerton Climb would challenge fans to swarm up to the top of the transmitter in the shortest time, with prizes as well as fame for the surviving competitors. Thinking how huge crowds always turned out for public executions and death-defying stunts in times past, the event would surely put the Island on the world-wide map. Another bonus would be that, unlike the proposed motor cycle 'Diamond Races' at our end of the Island, the only people at risk of death or grievous injury would be the competitors.

~

It's downhill all the way now, following an old shepherd's trail towards the outskirts of Newport.

Being so close to civilisation yet still in the deep heart of the countryside is another thing I like about this Island. Just across the water, the south coast is now one contiguous chain of roads and concrete proms dotted with towns and cities. Here, trees still reach down to the sea.

Portsmouth's Spinnaker Tower glitters distantly in the autumn sun, then my destination comes suddenly and strikingly into view. The two edifices could not represent the past and present better.

Some castles are not much more than piles of stone; others have been messed around too much for my liking. This one seems to be just about right.

There's enough left of the curtain walls and towers for you to screw up your eyes and get an idea of what it would have been like to arrive here the best part of a thousand years ago. Castles were meant to impress and intimidate as well as defend. In its lofty, towering setting, Carisbrooke certainly did and still does.

It's thought the Romans may have built a fortress here, but for sure the settlement dates back to Saxon times. Then, it would not have been much more than a wooden building surrounded by an earth mound and built to defend that part of the Island from Viking raids. By the time of Henry I, Carisbrooke was a proper castle, and extra fortifications were added much later in anticipation of the arrival of the Spanish Armada.

It was to Carisbrooke that Charles I was brought for safe keeping before his execution in 1649. His two daughters were held here after his death, and one died within its dank and oppressive walls.

I arrived on a school trip invasion, and all I can remember is a donkey and a giant hamster wheel. The original contraption was a device for drawing water from the well, and the wheel had to be turned 250 metres to summon up one bucket of water. Though not working for a living nowadays, the donkeys are still at hand. I hear that some Island law and order enthusiasts are said to be demanding a return to the original method of using prisoners to turn the wheel and entertain the crowds.

~

Talking of prisoners, as well as playing host to potentates, prelates and even nascent saints, it's also been home to some pretty evil men. The Kray Twins, Moors Murderer Ian Brady and the Yorkshire Ripper all served time at the once-notorious Parkhurst Prison.

Starting life as a military hospital, it became a children's prison in 1838, and despatched a total of fifteen hundred boys aged between twelve and eighteen years of age to colonies in Australia and New Zealand. As a prison for young offenders, Parkhurst was subject to fierce criticism for its harsh regime, including the use of leg irons.

Nowadays, ninety-eight percent of the inmates of the now-named Camp Hill are sex offenders, but I see from the local paper that we are to expect the arrival of a man as infamous and even more deadly than his most notorious predecessors.

Radavan Karadzic became known as The Butcher of Bosnia and has been sentenced to life imprisonment for genocide, war crimes and crimes against humanity, including the 1995 massacre of more than eight thousand men and boys at Srebrenica.

At 75, Karadzic is more than likely to breathe his last inside the walls of Camp Hill. I often walk in Parkhurst Forest, and it seems a suitably just additional punishment that the Butcher of Bosnia will live and die just metres from the freedom and light of such a glorious open space.

∞∞∞∞

A Wondrous Isle

Babylon may have had its Hanging Gardens and Giza its giant pyramid, but let us not forget the seven wonders on offer on the Isle of Wight.

Needles *you can't thread. ...*
Ryde *where you walk. ...*

Newport *you can't bottle. ...*
Freshwater *you can't drink. ...*
Cowes *you can't milk. ...*
Lake *where there's no water. ...*
Newchurch *that's old. ...*

16

"There was a Young Lady of Ryde,
Whose shoe-strings were seldom untied.
She purchased some clogs,
And some small spotted dogs,
And frequently walked about Ryde."

One of Edward Lear's lesser-known limericks.

'So what's this with talking as if you're chewing a brick? Is that your idea for how Sergeant Westfield should speak? I suppose if the director can't hear what you're saying, he won't know that you've got your lines wrong. Is that the idea?'

'Thrs nt itatll..' I said in injured tones.

'Beg pardon?'

'I said,' I said, 'that's not it at all. I'm practicing talking without moving my upper lip.'

'Why? Your character's not a ventriloquist in his spare time, is he?'

'Har-de-har,' I replied with some bitterness of tone. 'I'm worried about my front tooth falling out before the shoot. I'm practicing a cover-up in case it does.'

'I see,' said my wife as if she didn't. Then, mock-compassionately: 'Would you like me to glue the wobbly one in?'

'No thanks,' I replied. 'You might glue my lips shut as well.'

She looked thoughtful. 'Never thought of that, dear heart.'

'Nt mch you ddn't...'

~

Mushrooms are funny things. One minute they're not there, then suddenly they pop up like, well, mushrooms. Not all are edible, and some deadly. In France, most provincial chemist shops offers a fungi-identifying service. Even so, thousands of people poison themselves every year.

While the window of opportunity is briefly open, I like foraging for chicken-in-the-woods, field mushrooms, puff balls or shaggy ink cap and pretending I am a real fungi sleuth. It adds to the pleasure of a walk on the wild side, but I limit myself to harvesting the half a dozen varieties of which I am sure. This morning I struck gold, or rather a happy hunting ground for fungologists.

Bouldnor Forest spreads across more than a hundred hectares, and is part of a nature reserve running along the coast east of Yarmouth towards the village of Shalfleet. It has a lot going for it, including, as the guide book's blurb has it, a Prehistoric Past.

The area is protected, but is pleasantly unkempt and looks as if it is generally left in peace by those in charge of protecting it. The guide book also says it's the only place on the Island to find a rare fern by the many small but swarming ponds, which are home to crested newts, toads and all sorts of exotic algae. I don't know if it's auto-suggestion because of what I've read, but bits of the forest and foreshore do have a sort of primeval feel, and on some early mornings with the mist rising and the sound of silence everywhere, you could be on the set of *Jurassic Park*.

Bouldnor is also a perfect example of another thing I like about the Island, which is how often trees reach almost to the water's edge. This makes it an extra delight to break through the treeline and arrive in little shingled coves with parts of what look like a petrified forest swaying in the murky waters.

Another unusual aspect of the Forest is that people still live in it, albeit in somewhat grander accommodation than eight thousand years ago.

Far from the road and a long way down some off-puttingly potholed and rutted tracks, million-pound palaces, tumbledown shacks and shanties exist in apparent harmony.

For people who don't want to put their home on show, it must be a delightful place to live if you have a 4x4 motor and a good memory when you leave its seductively green and silent embrace to do the weekly shop.

~

An hour on and I've struck really lucky.

Off the main and in a well-drained, shady clearing I literally almost stumbled on an almost perfectly symmetrical ring of parasol mushrooms. They're one of the largest varieties and utterly delicious. Like all foraged foods, they naturally taste better simply because they are free.

With a full bag, and having marked the spot for future foraging, I was walking back along the track when a figure appeared from behind a large oak. He was unusual in appearance even by Island standards, and could have been a young-looking old man, or an old-looking young one. He was exceeding short, narrow of shoulder and big of hip, with a florid face and a fringe of reddish hair above large, very ear-shaped ears. Around them were hooked a pair of wire framed spectacles of the type affected by Vladimir Lenin and John Lennon. I don't know if the Island has its equivalent of the Irish Leprechaun or Cornish Pisky, but if not, this man would certainly be in the running for the position.

In keeping with the image of a wood sprite or mischievous imp, he was also wearing the sort of other-worldly, almost smug expression as if he knew something the rest of the world did not. I have found it a look common to people who like to ingest any of the varieties of the marijuana plant. Altogether, and without too much effort, I could see him sitting on a toadstool mending a pair of pixie boots or counting the gold pieces in his crock.

On his own feet were a pair of very unsuitable patent leather pumps, and I saw he had chosen to wear shorts underneath his ragged knee-length gaberdine raincoat, or perhaps simply forgotten to put his trousers on. Apart from looking smug, he was whistling a tuneless tune as he guided a battered old pushbike along the track. A carrier bag hung from the handlebars, and as we drew level he stopped, pointed at it and asked in a reedy voice: 'D'you like mushrooms?'

I guardedly said I did, at which he took the bag off the handlebars and held it out to show the contents. It was filled with distinctively and brilliantly red-capped, spotted members of the amanita fungi family. Even with my limited knowledge, I can tell a deadly toadstool when I see one.

'Would you like some?' he asked with a gappy smile.

'Er no, you're alright,' I said. 'I've got loads here.'

I showed him the contents of my bag, after which he gave me an almost sympathetic look. 'They're okay,' he said, 'but not like these.'

'No,' I agreed, 'I can see that.'

It was an awkward conversation, as we seemed to be occupying a fractionally different part of time and space. He was not foaming at the mouth or exhibiting any overt signs of mental disorder; he just seemed to be partly in another place.

'Do you think some of them might be poisonous?' I asked, as tactfully as I could.

Another gappy smile and he shook his head. 'They're lovely,' he said, taking one out of the bag and holding it towards me. 'I've been eating them for years. You just dries them out and toasts 'em. Like chestnuts.'

I looked at the toadstool and the bag and him and thought how best I could handle this moral dilemma. Should I try and reason with him, or snatch the bag and save him from himself?

In the end and as usual I took the easy way out and watched as he walked away.

Thinking and talking about it with my wife, I could not see what else I could do. I couldn't see the police scrambling a helicopter if I alerted them to a man with a bag of toadstools. As for a physical approach, although small, he was younger than me and looked wiry, and for all I knew might have magical powers and I would not fancy spending eternity frozen into the shape of a petrified tree.

Overall, my wife agreed I had few options, but did not help my peace of mind when she suggested I keep an eye on the local paper for any tragic death-by-toadstool stories.

~

I like Ryde, though I'm not quite sure why. It's got a lot going for it, but also quite a bit not going for it.

In competition with Newport as the most populous town on the Island, Ryde sits sparkily on the coast, engaged in a staring match across the Solent with Portsmouth. In a smaller way, it has the same ills as my home city, but to me seems a bit sassier. It's without doubt a town with attitude as well as altitude. Architecturally and design-wise I find it a place with loads of style, although many Islanders (and even visitors) may disagree.

Unlike Portsmouth, Ryde largely escaped the attentions of the Luftwaffe and later the brutal attentions of a succession of mostly deranged post-war modernists. The town maintains some fine examples of Regency and Victorian architecture, boasts one of the longest piers in the United Kingdom and, unlike many south coast resorts, has wide swathes of sandy beaches when the tide is right. Like Portsmouth it can be an edgy sort of place, but that's only natural as bad drinkers, fighters, drug-doers, their suppliers and other not very nice people are naturally drawn to high population areas.

I suppose some older residents would regard Ryde and Newport as the Sodom and Gomorrah of the Island, but then most of them don't know just how bad it can get on the mainland.

~

I'm in Ryde for a medical examination to assure the producers of *The Beast Must Die* that I will be up to the stresses and strains of filming.

My examiner is a very tall, spare man who looked increasingly puzzled as he listened through his stethoscope, hit me with rubber hammers, peered at his instruments and put me through my paces like a vet checking if a really old horse was fit to continue working or should be sent to the knacker's yard.

Eventually, he asked me to put my trousers back on and sat, absent-mindedly tapping his teeth with a rectal thermometer as he scrutinised his clipboard.

'It's okay if it's bad news, doc,' I said bravely, 'I can take it.'

'No, you're fine,' he said, 'It's just that I've never examined anyone with so many ailments who's in otherwise such good nick. And I can tell you that you really shouldn't be.'

~

After the medical, I laboured up one of the breath-taking roads from the prom to the main shopping area. I was in search of a café where they would serve me a proper cup of coffee, which to me means hot water, simply seeped through grounds of a decent blend of coffee. That counts out any place favoured by women having an orgasm over something that looks like an over-the-top milk shake, and image-conscious, skinny, bearded blokes wearing man-buns and over-tight trousers. They will be either drinking or serving beverages which are twice the price they should be because they have a made-up name. In Italian, *latte* just means 'milk', but in saw-you-coming coffee shops it means 'bloody expensive'. It's fine by me if people want to pay through the nose for a cup of milky coffee just because it's the flavour of the moment, but don't expect me to join in the game.

I found my caff amongst a welter of charity and unfashionable clothing shops, and it looked just the job. Outside, a nice blue, red and yellow frontage as if the owners were using up some spare paint, and a plain, non-punny or smugly clever-clogs name above the door. There was also a blackboard advertising all-day breakfasts, with beans as well as mushrooms and black pudding as standard.

Inside, décor and clientele were equally reassuring. The modern version of lino on the floor, sensible plastic tablecloths and chairs and, best of all, no sign or sound of an espresso machine on the back counter. On the wall were the usual out-of-date posters, including one from the last century. Another unexpected delight was that the ketchup came in oversized plastic tomatoes with traditional gummed-up nozzles. The final winner for me was that the newest record on the juke box was Only Sixteen, a big and only hit in 1959 by the Isle of Wight's own Singling Milkman, Craig Douglas. I think the décor had just evolved over the years, but if the owner had called it 60s retro and served frothy coffee in see-through cups, I reckon she could have at least doubled the price of the all-day breakfast.

~

Another nice thing about characterful caffs is that they attract characterful customers.

At a table by the counter when I entered, a diminutive elderly lady in an oversized wrap-round raincoat, beret and trainers put me in mind of the great character actress Patricia Hayes as *Edna the Inebriate Woman.* On her lap she was nursing a tiny, rat-like dog, and was in animated conversation with a Larry Grayson lookalike in blue Breton fisherman's cap and a white safari suit.

At a nearby table, a young couple were working hard to look bored and resentful at the same time. They were pitch-perfect in their late 1970's punk personas, complete with Mohican hairstyles and black eyes and lips. What I couldn't know and did not like to ask was whether they were ahead of the fashion times, or really seriously behind them in a very isle of Wight way.

As I compared the relative virtues of hash browns or chips before deciding to have both, the bell clanged and the net curtain flapped as the door swung open and a very, very small man strode purposefully in. He reached up and held on to the door handle as a giant figure appeared on the threshold. He was at least six feet and I would guess almost as round, and was walking with the aid of a hugely carved staff that would have made Gandalf jealous.

The couple made for the table next to mine, the big man sitting with his back to the aisle and the little man clambering up onto a chair with two cushions stacked on it. Both nodded and smiled in my direction and waved to the other customers in a lovely all-inclusive gesture.

Their breakfasts arrived before mine, which seemed only right and proper. Contrary to my expectations, the waitress/owner/chef put the Extra Big Breakfast in front of the little man, and a small plate of scrambled egg, bacon, mushrooms and toast in front of Gandalf.

They set to, the big man taking a delicate and even bird-like approach, the little man attacking his own plate with gusto and even reaching over to steal a piece of toast or a forkful of egg.

As my MBB (Monster Big Breakfast) arrived, we fell to talking, and my dining companions said how happy they were to have relocated from the mainland. After London, they had tried living in Portsmouth but had felt just as lost there, while in Ryde they could be themselves and fit in. It was, they said, like a big village filled with interesting and creative people, and unlike anywhere they had lived on the mainland, including and especially Brighton.

Here, said the small man, waving the sausage on

his fork to make his point, you could be yourself without trying to be someone else to gain approval. Ryde had its bad bits, but was still somewhere very special, and definitely somewhere with a good heart.

Although close to the road in and out of Ryde, there's an air of calm as soon as you turn into the gates of Quarr Abbey.

The Abbey was founded in 1132 by a Cistercian order of 'white monks'. The brothers lived a life of contemplation and devotion, but also worked the land, maintained the bridge at Wooton, the tide mills and salterns (for gathering salt from the nearby shore) and even help fight off the occasional marauding party of brigands.

Their lives went along smoothly enough until 1536 when the Abbey fell victim to Henry VIII's greed and spite. The buildings were torn down and the stone sold off, some of it for use on Yarmouth Castle.

The consecrated ground lay fallow until the turn of the 20th century, when the modern buildings were built to accommodate a small number of exiled Benedictine monks, fleeing from religious intolerance in France.

Nowadays, it's a pleasant place to visit and enjoy, with woodland walks, a tea garden, and a visit is all the more enjoyable because parking is free.

The bells were announcing the start of the mid-morning mass as I arrived. Inside the upturned boat of unpleasingly modern brick, the congregation totalled one. My heart lurched as, from behind, the diminutive figure in a sensible trouser suit and neat golden helmet of hair looked just like my mother of forty years before.

Feeling irrationally as if I had no right to intrude, I picked up a candle, put a pound coin into the offerings box and turned to leave.

As I lit the devotional candle, a door opened and it seemed it would be rude for me to leave as a small procession emerged into the aisle.

Walking in pairs, two of the brothers wore white robes, while two were in black. In between one pair was a man in shirtsleeves his rolled-up sleeves and braces contrasting oddly with the robes. He was probably a novitiate, but hemmed in and arms stiffly at his side, he looked like a prisoner under escort.

Reaching the transept, one of the white monks sat beside the altar as the others took places in the stalls or aisle. When they had settled, the obviously senior white monk raised a hand and led the others in a singing chant which soared to the rafters and, perhaps because the beauty of the sound contrasted so much with the ugly brickwork, it literally made my skin tingle.

I am not a religious person and only go to church for weddings, and increasingly for funerals, but the sights and sound held me. I was so taken, I forgot to put the lit candle on a spike with the others, and burned my fingers. My grunt of pain did not distract the monks, but was enough to cause the single worshipper to turn. Quite irrationally, my heart stopped as I hoped to see my mother's face, but the lady was wearing a mask.

For the next hour the monks went through their ancient routine and sequence of prayer and chant and song and genuflection, and looked as if they meant it. I watched and thought it would not be such a bad thing to give oneself to a life of devotion and contemplation, away from the world and its harsh realities.

As the senior monk made his preparations and the elderly lady moved to the altar to accept the body and blood of Christ, I remember Will telling me how he had spent almost a year as a guest in a Benedictine monastery in deep France and on the banks of the River Loire. He said he had been truly at peace there, and would have stayed had they not thrown him out for stealing the cutlery.

Outside and strangely relaxed and contemplative, I scribbled some notes as I sat in the gardens under the stony gaze of the Madonna with baby Jesus in her arms.

As I wrote, the main door to the monastery opened and the sole member of the congregation came out. She had taken off her mask, and gave a slight smile and nod as she walked towards the car park. She looked not at all like my mother, but seeing her in the half-light as the monks' devotions soared towards the Heavens is an experience I will not forget.

∞∞∞∞

What's left of the original 12th century Abbey

Brothers at rest: The monks' cemetery at Quarr

Just along the shore from the Abbey is a fine example of how Island villages can keep their identity, even in the shadow of urban sprawl.

Though standing cheek-to jowl with noisy, attention-seeking Ryde, Binstead is a place of calm, and a visit really is like stepping back in time. Not centuries, perhaps, but a good few decades, and in a nice way. When the tide is right. I'm told you can walk along the unpretty but undisturbed shoreline, most of the way to East Cowes.

There's also an air of peace and tranquility about the graveyard at the Church of the Holy Cross, and it has a number of interesting residents. One is Samuel Landon, said to be the biggest man in the world at the time of his death in 1844. Nearby is a memorial stone to Tomas Sivell, mistaken for a smuggler and shot to death by Customs officers in 1785 while going about his business in the Solent. His wife had this telling admonition inscribed on the stone:

All you that pass, pray look and see;
How soon my life was took from me;
By those officers as you hear;
They spill'd my blood that was so dear;
But God is Good is Just and True,
And will reward to each their due.

~

Donella is painting in her studio and I am next door in the summerhouse, taking a break from my line-learning by catching up with what has been happening on the mainland and beyond.

On the front page of a national broadsheet is a picture of a fading but still beauteous film star. Alongside is the promise that inside we can learn how she keeps her cascade of Titian hair in such marvellous shape at the age of 70. In smaller type we are told that the latest Covid 19 Deaths and Infections rate can be found on page 37.

The lead story in the local paper confirms that the belief that the Isle of Wight can be seen as a foreign country even by the most sophisticated of shops.

The article concerns the efforts of a local man to buy a runner-bean frame from Harrods. They responded by apologising that they were unable to fulfil his order as shipments to places outside the UK were temporarily suspended because of new Brexit rules.

~

As I learn about a dog which likes to surf in Freshwater Bay but has yet to try paragliding, my agent phones to remind me about my costume-fitting appointment next week. She asks how I am getting on with my lines, and I tell her I am word-perfect.

The truth is that I do know my lines; my problem is saying them.

My first scene is when I poke my head into the chief of detective's office, nod respectfully and say:

'Sir, we're here to collect DI Gerrity's things. For his wife.'

What I find myself saying is:

'Sir, 'Just to say we've come to pick up D.I. Gerrity's stuff. It's for his missus. Awight?'

I know what I should say, but can't stop myself changing the dead detective's name to Haggerty or Foggarty or, most commonly, Rafferty. I also can't resist editing the lines to fit more easily into my mouth and what I think my character would more likely say in his gruff, Sarf London accent. Without any conscious decision, Sgt. Westfield has become a strange tri-brid of Ray Winstone, Bob Hoskins and Danny Dyer.

I suppose my involuntary going off-script comes from me being a time-served editor and dialogue writer, but I don't think the director or -especially-the person who wrote the words would be best pleased at my creative tinkering. I want to say the words exactly as they are written down, but can't. And the more I try the worse it gets.

Another walk in the woods, and another character to add to my collection of interesting Wighteans. Because of my encounter, I've also solved the mystery of the Toadstool Man. He is, I am glad to hear, neither dead not mad, just a fan of hallucinogenic fungi.

I was exploring a large patch of woodland near Calbourne, and felt a definite atmosphere in the densest and permanently twilit depths.

Perhaps it was because this part of the Island, and in particular this ancient forest, is said to have had a long acquaintance with white witchery. Indeed, some residents claim that covens were being held here in the woods within living memory…and some say they still are.

It was Forestry Commission land so not marked, and the climb got steeper as the trees grew closer together. As I ventured deeper, the bird song died away and other sounds reached my ears. No ghostly voices or witch-like cackles, just unexplained sounds.

After a mile I could see no break in the trees or end to the forest, the light was fading and the hairs on the back of my neck bristling. It seemed it would be a good idea if I gave up and turned back. That proved not to be as easy as it should have been.

I had used my usual device when in unfamiliar and unmarked woodland trick of registering each time I left the track with an arrow made of dead wood. This is fine if you don't stray too far from the last marker and there are only a few paths. My problem was that I could not find the most recent arrow, and without it I was lost. For sure, it was not where I thought I had left it. Just for a moment I wondered if someone could have moved it. Then I reminded myself that one tree looks much like another. My main problem was that the sun had disappeared and I always forget whether it is the north or south side of tree trunks moss is said to grow. I consoled myself by thinking that getting lost here in unfamiliar surroundings was not as bad as on home territory a mile from my back door.

My phone was charged, but apart from the humiliation of calling the Emergency Services, I would not have been able to tell them where I was.

I had hunkered down and reached for my near-empty coffee flask when a very big dog came crashing through the undergrowth towards me. It was a strange mix of Staffordshire Terrier and Alsatian, and followed by a tall figure dressed in knee- length military boots, camouflaged combat coat and trousers. He was carrying a metal detector and a sharp-looking spade. Fortunately, both he and his dog turned out to be of amiable disposition. We got talking, and I found I had chanced upon not only a caulkhead, but one whose forebears had occupied the Island since Viking times.

Kingslayer told me he had been looking for interesting artefacts, and in his spare time was a member of a Viking re-creation group. He also knew about fungi, and was familiar with the toadstool collector I had met in Bouldner Forest. My new friend explained how, before going on a raping and pillaging expedition, his Viking ancestors would feed deer with toadstools and then drink their urine. It put them in a suitable wild mood and was where the term 'Berserker' came from. Dingbat - the hobgoblin I met in the forest- did not, as far as Kingslayer knew, process his toadstools through deer. Rather, he cooked and took small pieces at regular intervals, and had built up a resistance. Either that, or Dingbat was, as a lot of locals thought, a truly magical creature from another time or planet.

Relieved to hear Dingbat was alive if not well, I pretended to know where I was, and followed Kingslayer and his dog to the nearest road. As we parted, I promised I would come to the next meeting of the Viking group, which would be a training session at Wooton Scout Hall.

~

My teeth are wobbly but still in place and I have been for my costume fitting.

It was surprising how, as I dressed, I actually felt more confident in my ability to portray a veteran police sergeant. The tunic and hat fitted perfectly, though the trousers were several inches too big around the waist. Although I did not admit it to my dresser, this was because vanity had prompted a diet. It is well known in the business that television adds at least ten pounds to your appearance, and my cruising weight is at least twenty pounds more than what it should be.

The fitting lady took some shots of me in costume, and nodded her approval. She was obviously more concerned with my costume than my looks, so I will have to wait until shooting day to see if the director thinks a man in his eighth decade can pull off the role of a serving policeman, even on the Isle of Wight.

17

"...you can imagine what happens when a mainland species gets introduced to an island. It would be like introducing Al Capone, Genghis Khan and Rupert Murdoch into the Isle of Wight. The locals wouldn't stand a chance."

Hitchiker's Guide to the Galaxy author Douglas Adams.

As Tennyson's Victorian influencer John Keats put it so poetically, we are at the time of mists and mellow fruitfulness.

The changes from season to season are nowhere near as dramatic in town, but much more apparent when you have the countryside outside your back door.

As the days grow bleaker, wild creatures dig in and

prepare for hard times as best they can. Wild flowers wither and die, but will live again next year. We stock up on tins and provisions as if the Co-op was not just down the road, dig out our winter clothing and watch the autumn leaves fall like snow from the line of oaks alongside the fence. In some ways it is sad to see the dying of the summer's light, but I like the way the seasons let us know of their arrival and passing. As well as older, it makes one feel more alive.

~

In case you ever need to know, a two-gallon Low Price plastic bucket from B & Q's Newport (or, I presume, any other) branch holds between five and seven hundred dead oak leaves. That's according to how firmly they are compacted, I should not need to add.

So far this week I've filled forty-seven buckets and emptied them over the fence. Technically speaking the leaves belong to the owner of the trees from which they fall, so I am returning his property.

The leaf-gathering and dumping also helps occupy my time and mind as it is now only days before I put on my peaked cap, tunic and clown-waisted trousers to walk in front of the cameras as Sergeant Westfield. I realise my wife is right when she says I am like an over-trained boxer, but can't stop myself going over and over my handful of lines. According to Donella, I even say them in my sleep. She adds that I deliver them much better when unconscious than awake, which is not much help.

~

Friday, and I walk up to Golden Hill Fort and then along the shore to the village to pick up a copy of the local paper. I could have it delivered or read it online for free, but I feel I'm acting improperly if I don't take the long route and buy a copy from Che Guevara's shop. It's part of the Island effect, perhaps.

As usual, I stop on the way back to share the latest news with Ent the fallen tree. The occasional dog or its owner leaves the track to investigate, but don't stay long when they see an obviously mad old man reading the stories out aloud.

~

Here we go.

It's just after six on a wet, windy and dark Monday morning. I am being whisked to Newport to be got ready for what may be the start of a late but rewarding acting career. Or a sudden end to it if I cock up my lines, freeze or have a nervous breakdown while in centre stage.

Laid on just for me, the chauffeured vehicle is not a stretch limo, but a gleaming people carrier. We are whipping along a series of alarmingly winding lanes, and I reckon this is because the driver knows, or thinks he knows, a short cut. If so, he is wrong, but it is a dramatic and thankfully distracting ride. Roadside trees appear for an instant in the main beam, their long shadows skittering across the tarmac as if fleeing our approach. It has a strangely hypnotic, strobe-like effect, and I shut my eyes and shake my head to allow me to concentrate on my silent mantra of endlessly repeating my lines.

I was in bed before ten last night and slept little;

now I am wide awake and there is a heightened awareness of place and circumstance and even destiny as I rush to meet my fate. Without putting it too strongly, my feelings might not be too dissimilar to those experienced by the unfortunate aristos being taken by tumbril to meet Madame Guillotine at the height of The Terror.

I hear a thinly disguised snigger and see the driver has turned to look at me over the back of his seat and in spite of speeding along such a dangerously dark and undulating lane.

"Is that your first line?' he says in a knowing way, and I realise I have been speaking aloud.

'Yes,' I reply casually, 'it's a good luck routine with me; you know, like a soccer player putting the same boot on first.'

'Ah,' he says in a tone that shows he doesn't believe me and knows I am shaking with nerves. 'Let's hope it works okay then, eh?'

~

I'm in my trailer, which is like a small caravan with lots of rails and clothes hangers and a full-length, illuminated mirror. My character's name was on the door, which made me feel even more nervous. Not for me the anonymity of a crowd scene. I am a proper actor and will be expected to act like one. Not an extra who would just have to lurk about and do what he is told, but someone who will be the very centre of attention from the camera crew, sound team, standers-by and, of course, the director himself.

When I arrived on set, the very nice production assistant ticked off my name on her clipboard and showed me to my trailer. She rather bemusedly took the box of chocolates I gave her to say thanks for all her help, and said she would deliver the other two to Make-Up and Costume.

My uniform was waiting inside, and now I am dressed I feel a bit better and 'in part' as actors like to say. The trousers are still at least four inches too big around the waist, but there are a pair of police-issue braces attached to them.

I've been trying out different types of walk towards the mirror for when I arrive at the C.I.D. Inspector's office and it hasn't gone well. I learned to walk a long time ago, but find myself so conscious of what I am doing that I'm stumbling like a child on his feet for the first time.

As I try to stop my knees colliding or spreading apart as if I am sitting on an invisible motorbike, the nice production assistant lady arrives with coffee.

'Make-up's ready when you are,' she says brightly, then frowns and asks if I have hurt my leg.

'No,' I stammer, 'just practicing my walk.'

'Ah, I see,' she says, with an expression that shows she doesn't, but is far too polite to say so.

~

I am ready to go.

Beyond a combing of my eyebrows, a re-parting of my hair a dab of something vaguely flesh-coloured to cover a few old scars and new zits, I do not bother Make-Up much. I don't know whether to be pleased that they think I look the part with so little attention needed, or to feel disappointed that I will not have a mask to hide behind.

~

I'm on set, and it's like a scene from a dystopian science-fiction movie.

Dawn is still an hour away, and the fierce lights on the goalpost gantries make the sheeting rain appear to be on fire as it drums down on the trucks and vans and fake police cars lining the quayside. Lines of thick cable writhe snake-like across the concrete, and figures scuttle to and from caravans and the entrance to the gaunt, concrete building. Inside, it is pretending to be a police station but is actually a disused barracks on the waterfront at East Cowes.

We costumed and privileged cast members make a dash across the yard, each escorted by an umbrella-wielding member of the production team. I have been given my personal assistant, who for some reason is dressed as one of the Super Mario brothers.

Inside, the building is even more abandoned-looking, but the first floor has been transformed into a busy office. On either side of a wide aisle, desks are littered with piles of paper and stained coffee mugs and the odd pair of handcuffs or other piece of police kit. I have been inside a few police stations and it looks very convincing.

~

I have met the director and he is a clown.

I don't mean this critically, but literally, as it is Halloween, and, like my Mario brother attendant, all the production staff are wearing some sort of costume. Spider Man is manning a set of lights near the ceiling, and Frankenstein's monster is guiding the camera along its rails. Hearing the director is going to be a problem for me, and is a double problem as he's also wearing a Covid mask. This means I won't be able to read his face and see what I think he thinks of my performance. But, after a few exchanges, he seems a nice man and certainly not the martinet I feared. It might even be that I can smuggle in a few improvisations and even improvements to my lines, but I will try and stick exactly to the script to start with.

~

My first scene is, thankfully, a non-speaking one, so I'll be able to ease myself into the part before I have to open my mouth. As the director explains, I will be seen in the background as the senior police officer character walks down the aisle to his office. He goes on to say, with his assistant repeating his words in sympathy for my hearing problem, I'm to be working at my desk, pointing out some detail on the computer screen to a visiting officer.

We rehearse the scene several times, then the assistant director shouts for quiet and it's action time. A veteran of extra work and having made fleeting appearances in *Worzel Gummidge, Doctor Who* and other seminal TV productions, I know I will need to resist the temptation to ham it up. Upstaging is not uncommon even amongst major film stars, and Steve McQueen famously infuriated Yul Brynner in *The Magnificent Seven* by fiddling with his hat, rubbing his jaw and shading his eyes from the sun when Brynner was speaking in the foreground. I don't think that's why so many extras over-do facial expressions, eye-rolling and arm-waving; they're probably just trying to help make the scene work. Knowing what goes on has spoiled my enjoyment of many a soap opera, as I can't resist studying the background artists as they raise eyebrows, frown, smile inanely or openly gurn as if suffering from St Vitus Dance.

I keep this in mind, and minimise my actions as the scene is filmed. After a final take, the director comes over to my desk and my heart lurches and I fear he is going to tell me to calm it down and stop playing to the camera. In fact, he says he likes what he sees and has an extra cutaway shot for me. This is always good news, and usually means that the man in charge wants viewers to see more rather than less of you. When the detective has passed and disappeared into his office, I am to lean out into the aisle and look thoughtfully towards the door. That will literally set the scene for when I arrive at his desk to deliver my come-to-collect-D.I.-Gerrity's-things lines.

We rehearse and then film the action, and the director announces himself satisfied with the first take. I should be flattered, but am in truth a little disappointed that I won't get the chance to try a range of other expressions or mannerisms or discuss how I can improve the scene with my director.

~

I once heard a big-time and monumentally precious actor comparing his craft with war. For the participants, It was, he said, hours of boredom and then moments of intense action and sometimes terror. Hardly an appropriate comparison, but I can see what he was getting at. The past four hours have been occupied with ten minutes of filming and the remainder rehearsing or sitting in my trailer.

Five hours on and I have still not uttered my opening line, but suddenly Super Mario is at the door. It is time for the moments of terror.

~

Before we rehearse, the director asks me if I know my lines, which seems an odd question. Then, his assistant says it's time for action.

When they have crouched down out of shot in opposite corners of the office, the cameraman has adjusted his lens and someone has called for silence, I get my cue and walk into the lion's den.

As practiced a thousand times, I lean forward, tap the door with the back of my hand and push it open. Or that was the plan. In fact, I should have pulled rather than pushed, and end up with my face squashed against the glass panel in the door like a little boy looking into a sweet shop window.

We go again, and after I take a firm grip of the waistband of my clown trousers and do my stuff, there is silence as everyone in the room looks at the director. I hold my breath as he looks down at his hand-held monitor. After a moment, he looks at me and then at his assistant and then smiles and nods as if to say: 'He'll do.'

When I have come down from a rush of relief that borders on hysteria, I become a spectator for the rest of the afternoon. Perversely, and now I have got through my opening lines, I wish I had more to say. Much more.

~

Shooting is over for the day; the arc lamps dim and

die and the posh people-carrier whizzes me home. I can't wait to tell my wife how well the day went, and how silly she was to worry about how my performance would go down. I know I'm never going to be a romantic lead or action hero, but I can see that an actor's life could certainly be for me. As she will doubtless remind me, if I do become a world-celebrated movie star, it will be because she persuaded me to come and live on the Isle of Wight.

∞∞∞∞

"This royal throne of kings, this sceptred isle.
This earth of majesty, this seat of Mars.
This other Eden, demi-paradise,
This fortress built by Nature for herself,
Against infection and the hand of war,
This happy breed of men, this little world,
This precious stone set in the silver sea,
Which serves it in the office of a wall,
Or as a moat defensive to a house,
Against the envy of less happier lands,
This blessed plot, this earth, this realm
... this Isle of Wight."

With apologies to Wm. Shakespeare, but anyone who knows the Island well would accept that his immortal lines apply particularly well (and maybe even better) to the Rough Diamond.

Across the country, Christmas has been put on hold, and that now includes the Isle of Wight.

The Island has been suddenly and dramatically demoted from the lowest to the highest level of infection ranking, and we actually have a worse rating than Portsmouth. Nobody can account for the surge, but there's a lot of muttering about holidaymakers and second-home owners bringing the bug over along with their money.

Something else that has been put on hold or possibly ended before it began is my acting career. I have joined the ranks of formerly successful film producers, directors and actors, and all because of a throwaway line about my baggy pants. If it didn't hurt so much it would be laughable, and I am still coming to terms with how long and hard I worked to make a success of my small part in the TV serial, and yet how quickly I, like Christmas, have been cancelled.

My agent phoned as I was packing for the second day's filming to say I had been dropped from the production. It was not my acting, she said, she had been told, but because I had made an 'inappropriate' remark concerning my clown-waisted trousers to the young woman who had been holding them up while the sound man fitted a microphone transmitter under my shirt. Thinking about it, I admitted that with the rest of the cast and the production team looking on, I had come up with a throw-away line which raised a moderate laugh.

Apparently, my agent said, my gag had so traumatised the young woman that she was unable to carry on with her work that day. There was, the production company's representative said, no right of reply or challenge to the termination of my contract, and I could not even offer an apology to the woman as she did not want to set eyes on me again. I would be paid for my work and another day's fee in compensation for lost income. If I appeared in the final cut, I would get an on-screen credit.

As ever when there is unexpected and bad news, my wife and I went down the pub. When I looked glumly into my glass and said I had opened my mouth and put my foot in it yet again, Donella squeezed my hand and said it did seem strange that a grown woman in that field of work should be traumatised by hearing a man old enough to be her grandfather talking about his trousers. Perhaps it was a little Les Dawson-ish to say how long it had been since a young woman had fiddled with them, but considering what the 'victim 'must see and hear in an average working day, her reaction did seem more than somewhat extreme.

Perhaps it would be best, she concluded, to look on the bright side and assume that the real reason the company had got rid of me was not because I'd made an inappropriate remark. Perhaps, said my wife brightly, it was because they realised when they saw me in the flesh that I was so obviously far too old for the role. Or perhaps it was that my acting was really bad, or a combination of both.

∞∞∞∞

Epilogue:

I'm sitting deep in the heart of the Golden Hill woodland, getting my fallen tree friend up to date with recent events. To mark the occasion, I've brought a bucket of Kentucky Fried Chicken for the fox family, and included a couple of packets of roasted peanuts in the badger's supper pail. Later, my wife and I will see the new year at what could be a very interesting and unusual knees-up.

Knighton Gorge Manor was the home of one of the assassins of Thomas Becket, and believed to be cursed for eternity because of Hugh de Morville's mortal sin. As if to confirm the legend, a series of tragedies including suicide, violent death and fatal diseases afflicted subsequent owners. Following destruction in a fire set by the last owner in protest at his daughter marrying a clergyman, all that remains of the Manor is the gate-posts. But in the best tradition of spooky tales, the grand house is said to re-appear every New Year's Eve as midnight strikes.

Lights from ten thousand candles blaze from the windows, carriages carrying honoured guests rattle down the drive, and there's even a ghostly horseman who re-enacts his suicide over gambling debts by riding into the lake. As this is claimed to be the most haunted place in Britain, it will be a suitably Isle of Wight-ish way to say goodbye to the old year.

The course of the pandemic in the new year will determine when we will be able to return to foreign parts, including the mainland. As it has turned out, we, or rather my wife, certainly chose a good place to be during the lockdown.

For sure it has been a remarkable year of discovery of the Island, and to some extent, myself. The house and garage still resist the urge to become one, and I know my wife would be happy to spend the rest of her life here. In spite of my initial reluctance, I can see the attraction.

This remarkable isle may not be sceptred, but it is set in a sometimes-silver sea and, rough diamond or not, it's certainly a precious stone. It's also been a royal throne for many a king and queen, and I don't think calling it a demi-paradise is over-stating the attractions of this unique and sometimes mind-numbingly beautiful part of the kingdom.

I admit I had my doubts about the potential joys of spending any amount of time here, but, thanks to my wife, I came, saw and was certainly conquered. Or, to paraphrase another professional explorer:

Veni, Vidi, Vectis.
(With apologies to J. Caesar)

Bibliography

Wight-Biography of an Island by Paul Hyland, published by Dovecote Press

Walking on The Isle of Wight by Paul Curtis, pub: Cicerone

Isle of Wight Short Walks by David Foster, pub: Pathfinder Guides

The Little Book of the Isle of Wight by Jan Toms, pub: The History Press

A Dictionary of the Isle of Wight Dialect by William Long, pub: Forgotten Books

Original Ghosts of the Isle of Wight by Gay Baldwin, pub: Gaynor Baldwin

Personae Vectenses: Isle of Wight Notables by Phillip Armitage, pub: Beachy Books

Isle of Wight Pubs by Philip Christian, pub: PiXZ Books

On-line and On-air

Isle of Wight Nostalgia:
http://www.invectis.co.uk/iow/people.htm

Fountain International Magazine
http://www.belinusline.com/

Isle of Wight County Press:
https://www.countypress.co.uk/

Island Echo: **https://www.islandecho.co.uk/**

Isle of Wight Observer: **https://iwobserver.co.uk/**

Isle of Wight Guru:
https://www.isleofwightguru.co.uk/

Isle of Wight Radio: **https://www.iwradio.co.uk/**

The Island Radio: **https://theislandradio.co.uk/**

Printed in Great Britain
by Amazon

85481872R00200